Practical Counselling an Helping

Practical Counselling and Helping is a practical, virtually jargon-free guide, offering clear information on the difference between counselling and helping, their limitations, and how they may be put into practice.

The book includes chapters on:

* What is counselling and helping?
* Basic counselling and helping strategies
* Handling difficult situations
* Further personal development

Drawing from a range of counselling methods, and offering a useful and detailed reading list, *Practical Counselling and Helping* will appeal to all students in the health professions and to all those requiring a clear account of how they might improve their own communication skills.

Philip Burnard is Professor and Vice Dean at the School of Nursing Studies, University of Wales College of Medicine, Cardiff.

Practical Counselling and Helping

Philip Burnard

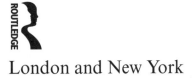

London and New York

First published 1999
by Routledge
11 New Fetter Lane, London EC4P 4EE

Simultaneously published in the USA and Canada
by Routledge
29 West 35th Street, New York, NY 10001

©1999 Philip Burnard

Typeset in Times by Routledge
Printed and bound in Great Britain by Biddles Ltd,
Guildford and King's Lynn

British Library Cataloguing in Publication Data
A catalogue record for this book is available from the British Library

Library of Congress Cataloguing in Publication Data
Burnard, Philip.
Practical counselling and helping / Philip Burnard.
p.   cm.
Includes bibliographical references and index.
1. Counselling. 2. Helping behaviour. I. Title.
BF637.C6B825   1999   98–49632
158'.3–dc21   CIP

ISBN 0–415–18883–0

For Sally, Aaron and Becky

Contents

Preface

Counselling gets a mixed press. Broadsheet and tabloid papers often run articles on the 'dangers of counselling'. We read how 'counsellors were standing by' after a national or local disaster. New age writers sometimes claim counselling as a panacea for a wide range of problems. Others refer to counselling as a form of personal growth.

There are already numerous, well-written books about counselling. The aim of this one is to simplify and demystify the process of counselling and helping. It does not, purposely, offer a particular theoretical position about people or counselling (although these are referred to in the text). The book is broadly based on the following assertions – all of which can and will be debated in the text:

- Counselling can help some but not all people.
- There is no one, particular, way of doing counselling.
- Although there are various theories about how human beings 'work', none has the monopoly on the truth about people.
- You don't necessarily need a huge amount of theory in order to help other people.
- There are certain skills that can be learned that can improve the way you help people.
- As in many things, simple forms of help are often more useful than more complicated ones.
- It is important not to frighten or mystify people when you try to help them.
- You do not have to 'psychologise' in order to help people.

This is a pragmatic approach to counselling. The book is aimed at anyone who wants to consider how they might help other people through talking with them. The aim is not to turn people into amateur psychologists or psychiatrists but to demonstrate that a few basic principles can help us to improve our dealings with others. The aim is also to show the limitations of all this. We cannot help everyone and we must know our limitations. We must also look after ourselves for if we invest heavily in helping others we may find the job overwhelming.

Who the book is for

Although aimed at anyone with an interest in helping others, the book should also be of value to students on health-care courses of various sorts: medical, paramedical, nursing, social work and so on. It may also be useful to those who are considering being counselled or who are seeking out a helper. A list of the sorts of people that may find this book useful includes the following:

- those on counselling training courses
- those thinking of going for counselling
- students on health-care courses
- volunteers
- the general reader who wants to know more about counselling.

What is in the book

The first chapter sets the scene. It contains a discussion about the nature of counselling: what it is and what it is not. It discusses the limitations as well as the advantages of counselling. In this chapter, I report what *counsellors* and *psychotherapists* see as the differences between what they do – as a means of clarifying what it is that counselling comprises and to differentiate it from psychotherapy.

Chapter 2 raises the question as to why we might counsel or help others. It may be self-evident that some people are attracted to doing counselling while others are not, it is still worth exploring the motives behind undertaking such an enterprise. The chapter also contains a discussion of how our own values are bound to colour the work we do in helping others.

The next four chapters describe and discuss various basic principles of counselling and helping and pay attention to issues such as dealing with 'difficult' situations and people. For, as we have noted, not everyone wants or can be counselled. The final three chapters focus on the counsellor. Chapter 7 is about looking after yourself as a counsellor, chapter 8 offers suggestions about further training and the final chapter offers a summary.

I have purposely avoided offering too many references to other people's work in the book. This is to make the text easier to read and avoids the 'hiccups' that often arise when people try to read pages of writing that are constantly interspersed with brackets, authors' names and dates. Where references are used, they are listed, in full, in the reference list at the end of the book. The final section – the bibliography – offers a detailed further reading list so that ideas in the book can be followed up. I have purposely included some classics in this list as well as more up-to-date books. Wherever possible, though, I have made sure that those classics are still in print.

Not referencing, in this way, leaves what is written open to debate and this, too, is part of the aim. My point is not to offer a definitive account of how counselling may or may not be done but to suggest ideas for debate. The finer points of theory can be found elsewhere and the bibliography will help in this direction.

During the writing of this book, I interviewed and talked to a range of counsellors, helpers and trainers and I have quoted their views, directly, in the book. Again, the aim is to keep the book contemporary and to offer practical views from those who work directly in helping other people. It is one thing to offer detailed theory in textbooks and another, perhaps, to listen to those who are in practice. I also report findings of various research projects that I have carried out concerned with clarifying the nature of counselling.

The book contains a mixture of theoretical debate and a discussion of practical skills. I believe that practice needs to be underpined by theory – although, in the end, in helping other people we nearly always have to take the pragmatic route and help them according to 'what works'. No one particular way of counselling or helping people is likely to help every sort of person.

I hope, more than anything, that this book 'clears the air' a little and points towards a simple and pragmatic approach to helping other people. Someone once remarked that 'simplicity is genius' and, in the domain of helping others, I think they were right.

Philip Burnard
Caerphilly
1999

Acknowledgements

As usual, I am grateful to many people for helping with this book. First, thanks go to my wife, Sally and to my children, Aaron and Becky for their love and patience. Thanks, also, go to a number of people who have helped shaped my thinking about counselling over the past twenty years. A short list would include: Paul Morrison, Deb Salmon, John Heron, Charles Bailey, Jim Richardson, Sandy Kirkman, Max Kyei and Bryn Davis.

I will not commit myself to the frequently quoted 'author's paradox' and say that I remain responsible for any mistakes in the text. I cannot be responsible for them if I don't know that they are there but certainly hope to put them right in future printings and editions.

1   What is counselling and helping?

Sometimes we act, go in and out, do this and that, and everything is easy, casual and unforced; seemingly it could all be done differently. And sometimes, other times, nothing could be done differently, nothing is unforced and easy, and every breath we take is controlled by some outside power and heavy with fate.

What we call the good deeds of our lives, the ones we find easy to tell about, are almost all of that first, 'easy' kind, and we easily forget them. Other acts, which we find hard to talk about, we never forget; they seem to be more ours than the others, and they cast long shadows over all the days of our lives.

Hermann Hesse, *Klingsor's Last Summer* (London, Paladin, 1988), p. 9

We all need help at times. When things are going well, we tend to forget what it is like when they are not. When they are not going well, we tend to concentrate on the details of our distress: the details can block the way back to our feeling at peace with ourselves. Counselling and helping, however they are viewed, may be options for helping us out of these difficult times. It would be wrong, I think, to assume that counselling 'cures' people. It can, however, help people to get things into perspective and free them up to take action in their lives.

What is counselling?

Counselling is such a widely discussed activity that it is easy to believe that there is something mysterious about it. It is almost possible to imagine that there are some people in the world who have greater insights into the human condition than others and that those who do counselling may fall into this group. I contend that, although counselling can help a lot of people, what is done under the heading of counselling is nothing particularly special. That is not to underrate it, nor to suggest that 'anyone can do counselling'. In a way, though, we all do counselling. We talk to our friends, families, colleagues and help them to puzzle out what they should do next. People ask us for advice and we try to do the best we can. Sometimes, we find that what the other person is talking about means that we are out of our depth – we cannot think of the right things to say. The aim of this book is to make those sorts of conversations – what might be called 'counselling conversations' easier.

This first chapter is one that opens up the debate about counselling. In this chapter, I quote directly from what other counsellors and trainers have said to me in various studies. I also raise various issues that are returned to later in the book. The aim of this chapter, then, is to set the scene: to begin a debate that is probably unending for, as I indicated in the preface, I do not believe that there is one, right way to counsel or to help. In the end, much is up to the individual who engages in these practices. He or she must not only clarify his or her thoughts and beliefs on the matter but must also develop his or her own style and pattern of working.

First, it is useful to distinguish between *counselling* and *counselling skills*. By counselling, I mean that process that a professionally trained counsellor engages in. Such a person is likely to have had a fairly detailed and lengthy training and may be registered with a national body such as the British Counselling Association. By counselling skills, I mean those activities that all of us can engage in to help people to work out what they might do next to improve the situation they find themselves in. Most of us can use counselling skills while only a few of us will become counsellors. This book is aimed at helping those people who want to help others through the use of counselling skills rather than at those who aim to become fully qualified counsellors – although there will be things in this book that will help the latter category.

It has to be admitted that the term 'counselling skills' is limiting. The term can give the impression that helping people involves a set of learned skills that are simply practised and improved over time. Helping people though counselling is clearly more complicated than this. We not only need to learn skills, we need to consider, at least, the following: the personal qualities we possess, the context of the helping relationship, the subject matter being talked about, our relationship to the other person, our own strengths and deficits as a person and so on. No one who uses counselling skills should do so mechanically. In the end, the counselling relationship is what counts: the way in which we relate to the person we are trying to help. Sometimes that relationship 'works' and we are able to help and sometimes it does not. The skills are those things that we use to try to enhance the work we are doing with the other person.

Counselling, of the sort described here, is about helping another person in a conversation in which the other person is the focus of that conversation and where our aim is to help as much as possible by problem solving and enabling the other person to draw on their own and others' resources in order to plan a course of action. For, in my view, counselling is nothing if it does not lead to action. We can talk as much as we like about our problems but if, in the end, our behaviour or actions do not change, then that talking is not likely to help us much. There are exceptions to this. Sometimes, the talking helps us to accept the position we are in. Usually, though, the talking is aimed at invoking a change of some sort. The degree of change can vary, from radical change, involving the breakup or development of a new relationship to minor change, involving a new way of dealing with a work problem. The range of issues covered in a counselling and helping relationship can be considerable. It is not just the 'big' problems in life that can be helped: it is also the day-to-day niggles that make life uncomfortable. Nor should we assume that counselling can help in every situation. In the paragraphs that follow, I identify some of the things that counselling can and cannot do. First, though, it may be useful to identify some of the things that counsellors do.

What do counsellors do?

Professionally qualified counsellors are likely to work in rather different ways to the occasional counsellor or the helper. The qualified counsellor is likely, first, to talk to the person to be counselled to establish if he or she, as a counsellor, can help this person. Second, he or she is likely to explain the way in which he or she 'works'. Professional counsellors are often, although not always, linked to a particular theoretical and practical framework. Some will work in a psychodynamic way while others will be 'client-centred' and these approaches, with others, will be discussed later in this book. It is important that the potential client is clear about how this particular counsellor works.

The qualified counsellor will also discuss issues such as fees, numbers of meetings, rights by both parties to conclude the relationship and so on. Once both parties have agreed that the client will enter counselling with this counsellor, the pair are likely to meet on a weekly or monthly basis over a period of time. Sometimes, the professional counselling relationship will involve more than one client at a time, for example, two people in a relationship may seek counselling help together.

This, then, is something of the professional counselling relationship. Over time, the client and counsellor develop a close relationship and talk through a wide range of issues. The pair may or may not seek to establish goals to work towards and the counsellor may or may not offer the client advice or interpretations. Again, much depends on the counsellor's particular way of working. At some point, either by a contractual agreement or by a sense that the time is right, the counselling relationship ends and the counsellor or client part company. This parting may be final or there may be an agreement, on both sides, to take a break in the relationship. Many professional counsellors will be prepared to accept a client back, later, for further counselling.

The type of counselling and helping relationship described in this book is of the more informal kind. There are many people – health-care workers, social workers, volunteers, friends – who are able to help others through listening and talking. Here, the accent is less on regular meetings and there may be no fee involved. However, such 'informal' helpers can still use many of the skills of the professionally qualified counsellor. As we have noted, there need be no particular mystique about this sort of counselling but it remains true that people can learn to help others more effectively. It probably also remains true that, in the end, some people will be better helpers than others. Any amount of training cannot totally change us as people. Our personalities and individual differences, our backgrounds and general disposition to other people all mean that some of us will be better placed to help some people than others and some people will be able to help more people than others.

Before we go any further, it will be useful to make another distinction – between counselling and psychotherapy.

What are the differences between counselling and psychotherapy?

To explore the common question about the differences between counselling and psychotherapy, I sought the views of health-care professionals and others either engaged in counselling or who taught counselling.

Definitions of counselling

Respondents offered various definitions of counselling. Sometimes, those definitions referred to the *purpose* or *application* of counselling:

I think that [counselling] is any kind of assistance in helping people to come to terms with an emotional or spiritual problem of any kind. It is not confined to mental distress or mental disorder. It can range from things like being in debt to having acute depression.

Another respondent offered much more of a 'textbook' definition and followed this up by suggesting some of the purposes of counselling.

Counselling is an activity in which one person is helping and one is receiving help and in which the emphasis of that help is on enabling the other person to find solutions to problems or to look at particular situations which they would like resolved. Or to enable them to live more resourcefully. It involves the development, by the counsellor, of a range of particular skills but more importantly the adoption of a particular stance or attitude towards the person being helped and that includes the person feeling valued and able to explore the way in which he perceives himself and his world and not to feel judged by the counsellor.

Yet another hinted at a 'contract' but was not clear on this issue. However, as we shall see, some respondents *did* feel that counselling was contractual.

I think counselling is an activity in which two people agree to meet under certain conditions. And these conditions may be overt and negotiated and include such issues as confidentiality and expected outcomes. It is very much an interpersonal activity and the counsellor is there to help the client address and possibly resolve issues that are personal and meaningful to that individual.

One respondent referred to the need for the counsellor to remain *ordinary*. The argument is that other people are likely to respond to us more readily if we do not attempt to assume a 'professional' front or one that is 'artificial' in any way.

For me, it is a means of just being with another person who may need to talk over problems, job difficulties, personal dilemmas and so forth. In much the same way as you talk things over with a spouse or friend. That *ordinariness*, if you like, is important in counselling.

Another respondent discussed counselling in terms of 'helping people to help themselves – a point that the respondent felt was echoed in the literature on the topic:

> Counselling is creating an environment in which people can explore the issues – whatever they are, whether it is a particular way of looking at life, a childhood issue, perhaps – in a supportive atmosphere. One official definition is 'helping people to help themselves' and I quite like that: I think it's a good synopsis.

The immediate, here and now and forward-looking focus was identified as a key feature by one respondent:

> I see counselling as being concerned with the 'here and now' and future orientation, whereas psychotherapy is trying to explain behaviours in terms of past remembered and unremembered events.

The 'problem-solving' element of counselling was highlighted by various respondents, as follows:

> Counselling is a process to encourage a client to deal with a problem through the help of a counsellor. For this to occur the client is required to talk about their situation. A counsellor will only be able to assist the client to understand the problem if there is effective communication between them. Active listening skills help the counsellor to establish a feeling of respect, empathy and genuineness in the client and so that the subconscious protocol is present and counselling can occur.

It is noteworthy that this respondent saw the 'feeling of respect, empathy and genuineness' as factors arising in the 'client'. More often, the literature identifies these as qualities to be attributed to the 'counsellor'. It is not particularly clear what the respondent means by 'the subconscious protocol'.

> Counselling, I think, has a similar goal as psychotherapy, which is to assist the client to function 'better' (whatever that means). But counselling to me is a more problem-oriented, solution-oriented, time-limited and fairly acute process. It can be more directive than psychotherapy in that the counsellor has a sense of answers/solutions to problem 1, 2, and 3 (or however many are on the list...),

and moves the client towards those answers/solutions, using a variety of fairly specific techniques (e.g., relaxation training).

I refer to counselling when the presentation is of a person's problem and the response is focused on enabling the person/client to explore or decide solutions to problems. This may include personal insights into the need for more global change and recognition of the potential value of deeper therapy.

The following definition seems to stress the need for closeness and empathy between the counsellor and the client – and the context of the relationship:

> At the heart of the counselling process is the communication of ideas from the client to the counsellor. Just as it is necessary to place the problems of the client into the context of their circumstances, it is important to put the words into their context before starting to discuss any quotation.

Quite a different tack was taken by another respondent who offered a 'broader' definition of counselling. This respondent also saw 'psychotherapy' as 'one intervention in counselling':

> A perception within my sphere of education is that counselling is to be used as a means to enable the student to conform to the norms of the society in which they find themselves. Even the justice system will see counselling in this role in the way it will order offenders to take counselling for their problems. Also there is a tendency to enrol volunteers with minimal experience and training to take on front end counselling....Counselling would include all the above as well as other interventions. Counselling would then be the practice, and psychotherapy is but one intervention by the counsellor.

Another respondent compared and contrasted counselling and psychotherapy using the criterion of 'depth' but acknowledged, also, that the distinction was far from straightforward:

> Generally, the convention is that counselling is 'surface' and psychotherapy is 'deep' – as a previous post indicated. This doesn't quite match up with reality (whatever that is). There is also the interesting distinction between counselling, psychotherapy and

therapy (minus the psycho-). Behaviour therapy can be quite superficial *or* it can effect quite dramatic (and profound) changes (not necessarily intended). Then again people like Windy Dryden [a British writer on counselling and psychotherapy] talk about behavioural and cognitive-behavioural counselling, as well as therapy.

'Distance' and 'closeness' were issues for two respondents and the first of the following suggested that friendship and counselling are virtually synonymous (except, perhaps, in terms of motive). This is disputed by the second respondent:

> There is no essential difference between conversation with a friend and counselling, except that the professional counsellor does it better, without bias, and for remuneration.

> The essential [thing] about counselling is that the counsellor distances him or herself from the subject, to attempt to provide objective evaluation and reflection of the subject's situation. That's why it can be such a difficult situation to 'advise' a friend.

The final quotation identifies the perceived 'merging' of counselling with psychotherapy, by one respondent, and introduces the notion of 'unconscious' thoughts and feelings. It should be noted, too, that many respondents saw considerable similarities between counselling and psychotherapy – both in terms of practice and also in terms of the literature. The point was made by one respondent that Carl Rogers described himself both as a counsellor *and* a psychotherapist. This is perhaps most obvious in his collection of essays *On Becoming a Person*. It is notable, too, that a considerable amount of the literature refers to both 'client-centred therapy' and 'client-centred counselling'.

> I believe counselling merges into psychotherapy, but in the latter one makes it overt to the subject that unconscious thoughts and feelings are being explored. As has been intimated in this discussion, the definition lies in the hands of the counsellor/ psychotherapist. But I think the therapist has to make a decision on what level the client/therapist interaction is being made overt.

Psychotherapy

There is plenty of contention about what does or does not differentiate counselling from psychotherapy. This was mirrored in the responses from respondents in the study.

> Psychotherapy specifically applies to a clinical and mental illness as opposed to the neuroses that run through society. Psychotherapy is done by psychotherapists (as opposed to counsellors) and who can be lay therapists or qualified ones. Whereas counselling can be done by a whole range of people, from priests to professional counsellors.

> I would guess that counselling would have a much more practical, everyday, problem-solving slant to it – grounded in the here-and-now. Whereas psychotherapy, for me, evokes ideas to do with Freudian psychology.

Another respondent hinted at the Freudian approach to psychotherapy without making the issue explicit.

> I would see psychotherapy as exploring the person's life at a much deeper level including the development of insight based on exploration of early development, parental influences and those things *may* come into counselling. In counselling they are brought in to understand a *particular* situation rather than to understand the client him or herself.

The idea of the 'here-and-now' arose in another respondent's interview.

> I perceive psychotherapy as being different in a variety of areas. Psychotherapists tend to be educated and trained within a particular school of practice. They tend to be in therapy themselves as part of their training. And they would claim to work with individuals at a greater depth. I see them working more in the 'there and then' than the 'here and now'....The term is bound up with certain political issues – such as it is seen as more complex and goes on for longer and entails perhaps greater exploration and commitment on the part of the client.

One respondent had personal experience of *both* counselling and psychotherapy and made few distinctions between them. This may be a particularly important contribution to the debate given that it comes from someone who has had first-hand experience of both sorts of 'therapy'.

I've had both psychotherapy and counselling as part of my on-going training. I can't say there seems to be that much difference. Some see psychotherapy as synonymous with psychoanalysis but I find it difficult to make that distinction. Counselling doesn't go as deep as psychotherapy. Psychotherapy is a bit of a status thing as well. But there are other sorts of psychotherapy – TA [transactional analysis] and so on. I don't know really, the distinctions are blurred.

What the 'status thing' was is not made clear in the interview and was not pursued by the interviewer. The respondent *seems* to be hinting at the idea that having psychotherapy may be viewed as engaging in a 'higher status' activity than would be the case with having counselling.

The problem-solving side of psychotherapy was described as follows:

The public perception is that psychotherapy is much more enabling of the person to achieve goals regardless of any understanding of their position and whether the goals are the ones that require to be achieved.

One respondent attempted to identify something of the 'range' of approaches to psychotherapy, thus:

It appears that psychotherapy is a relatively specific intervention and can be limited to concepts and techniques that grew from psychoanalytic models, the client-centred model, and more recently, the communication models. Many intervention approaches can be, and are therapeutic, but would not be 'psychotherapy' in this limited sense. These would include, but not be limited to educational techniques, persuasion modelling, direct reinforcement of behaviours and guidance.

Another respondent also suggested that it was 'counselling' that was the 'broader' activity and noted some of the problems with this fact:

Psychotherapy is often seen as specialist and proactive whilst counselling is a much broader church....In many ways this breadth has led to a devaluation of the skills of a counsellor as well as a misunderstanding of the role of the counselling process.

One respondent was keen to stress the 'work' and painful elements of psychotherapy:

Psychotherapy takes time and hard work. It takes commitment on the part of the client to be willing to look at often very painful issues, and I believe it takes great sensitivity and humility on the part of the therapist who can help to guide the client 'safely' through the process.

For one respondent, the difference between counselling and psycho-therapy appeared to be the 'length' of the relationship. Psychotherapy was also something to be undertaken 'delicately':

I think psychotherapy is more introspective for both the client and the therapist, and is an unfolding of a story in a very careful, delicate way. Counselling is a shorter story (still being careful and delicate, of course!) with a more action-driven outcome than psychotherapy. I refer to psychotherapy when the presentation is of the person him or herself with a view to more global exploration of his or her life. The focus then is on aspects of self with a view to personal change or personal insight. This may of course include reflection of the impact of such change on specific problems.

Others saw psychotherapy as being intimately related to self-concept:

Psychotherapy is – I guess – more concerned with effecting changes which result in a shift in self-concept, identity (or indeed anything connected with the 'self'). Therapy might – as Kanfer said – be just about helping people change. Counselling might 'just' be about helping people *feel* differently, although not neces-sarily behaving differently.

I see psychotherapy as a specific approach to dealing with issues; an approach that focuses on exploring the inner self of the indi-vidual (within the context of individual or group sessions), taking into account the past, the present and the future. The past includes memories, perceptions and dreams of experience. Psychotherapy assists the client in putting all of these pieces into some under-standable or at least tolerable framework so that the client can move forward in life. (This sounds a bit pompous, but I can't think of a more simple way to say it...)

Counselling and other sorts of conversation

As there were conflicting reports about what counselling and psycho-therapy are, then it seemed reasonable to try to define the boundaries of counselling in another way. To this end, respondents were asked what the differences were between counselling and *other* sorts of conversation. If counselling is a special kind of conversation (as opposed to, for example, simply talking things over with a friend), then it seems reasonable that those who do it should be able to distinguish between simply 'talking' about something and 'doing counselling'. One respondent saw the difference in terms of *structure* – the counselling relationship was a more structured one that the more informal conversation:

> The only difference that I can see is in their formal structure. If things can be achieved by talking to your friends in the pub then that's fine. Whereas counselling usually has some sort of formal structure involved. It is also a professional relationship in the sense of a counsellor and client where the counsellor is paid to counsel or listen.

It should be noted that *that* respondent viewed counselling as an activity that was paid for by the client. Other respondents described the differences in terms of the *roles* played out by the participants in counselling:

> In counselling you would expect that one of the people has a problem, a dilemma that they are facing and that tends to be the focus of the interaction. Whereas the other person is seen as a counsellor, helper or listener. In a normal conversation that state of affairs might apply but it might also not apply and there may just be small talk about any aspect of the person's life. If you build on that definitional difference the more professional the counsellor, or the more formalised the counselling, the greater the difference would be between the helper and the helpee in terms of power, status and so forth. For example, if I go along to a friend of mine and talk about work or home problems, I won't feel guarded about status or power or being exposed psychologically because in that relationship it is guided by the principles of friendship or collegial relationships.

> One is in the allocation of roles. That is the roles of helper and helpee. I think the specific aims of the conversation are to help. It is purposeful and directed towards helping and a counsellor has

no other motives other than to help. People have argued that one of the differences is that the more therapeutic a conversation it is, the more likely it is to acknowledge what is happening in the here and now – in this relationship.

For another respondent, the two types of interaction were often blurred. It was sometimes difficult to say what the difference was between counselling and 'ordinary conversation'.

I think that it is a difficult question because sometimes an ordinary conversation turns into counselling and a counsellor may use counselling skills in their conversational life. I also think that counselling skills can enhance conversation and perhaps thinking as we talk about this, counselling is a specific form of conversation. I think sometimes the differences can be small and that initial sessions of clients can be 'conversational'. But they move into a counselling arena. I suspect that conversation is more reciprocal in depth and content whereas counselling tends to be less so – particularly on the part of the counsellor.

On the other hand, another respondent was *very* clear about the differences and saw them in *contractual* terms.

Counselling has very specific parameters. There is a contract, you know how long you will meet and so on. It is a very specific type of conversation. And although some of the skills and things the counsellor may be demonstrating are similar to other conversations it is very *intentional*. It is not two-way as in other conversations. The focus in counselling is very much on the client. It is intentionally focused.

What this respondent did not explain was whether or not he felt that the contract was *implicit* rather than *explicit*. Presumably few counsellors or their clients draw up formal contracts. If, on the other hand, the contract is an *implicit* one, the question is raised as to whether or not the client fully understands the 'rules of the contract'.

Who does counselling?

It is important to know what sorts of people *do* counselling. Should they be *qualified*? Should they be 'professionals' and so on. There were various responses to this sort of question.

Essentially anyone can do counselling. But for the most part it tends to be either professional counsellors or people who have traditionally had a counselling role, such as doctors, nurses or priests.

People do counselling who are interested in other people and who are prepared to spend time with them, supporting them. Anyone could, in that respect, do counselling. Whereas in the more formal type of counselling, such as in the formal helping agencies, you get the doctors, the social workers, the lawyers, the bar tenders. Then there are the people who set themselves up as professional counsellors. I don't know people who work like that but I guess they exist.

I think that counselling could be done by anyone but is more likely to be done better by someone who has had the opportunity to develop specific skills and who has been able to explore some of his characteristics and things like warmth, genuineness etc. However, it is likely that many people already possess those qualities and therefore could be better helpers than people who do not. I think there is a danger in saying that counselling is the preserve of counsellors because that relates it directly to training and I am not sure there is any evidence to demonstrate that training really does make a difference.

One respondent made a distinction between those who do counselling as part of another professional role and those who do it as a full-time job.

I would argue that there is a range of professionals whose primary professional role is working with people such as teaching, social work, nursing, medicine and in which the aim is to help others and where often that help is given through the medium of some sort of personal interaction. The more that interaction is the sole means of helping then the more we move towards that situation being counselling. For example, in medicine we see the prescribing of treatment and the relationship is not the sole means of helping. Clearly, there are some whose role is only seen as counselling and who have no other agenda. They do not have an educational agenda, a teaching agenda – the work they do is whatever the client brings. We can say then that they have a 'pure' counselling role.

Most of the above respondents took the 'anyone can do counselling' approach. Others, however, wanted counselling to be more formalised and for counsellors to be trained.

> People who [do counselling] are qualified counsellors. Although there may be people who have not done a proper certificate or diploma but who do counsel from experience. There are elements of counselling and counselling skills that occur in a lot of caring conversations that are carried out by nurses. It would be wrong to 'counsel' somebody without their permission and without a contract because of counselling's potential power.

How counselling can be used

If counselling is a therapeutic activity, it seems important to know what sorts of things counselling can be used for. The following responses were drawn from a number of transcripts. One respondent addressed the issue as follows:

> There is a whole range of practical difficulties that can be helped by counselling, such as difficulty with study skills and getting into higher education, through to things like depression following bereavement, or neuroses or mental illnesses. There has been an expansion in the profession of counselling in recent years – you often get the situation where someone calls themselves a professional counsellor on the basis of a range of qualifications which carry no guarantee as to the likely effectiveness of that counselling. At the same time, people with a lot of experience – such as psychiatric nurses – would not, necessarily, have that qualification recognised as appropriate in counselling. I think there is a process of excluding people from counselling as an occupation going on, which is similar to the way in which nurses exclude other people from working in nursing – so that nursing adopted a professional strategy for excluding people and counselling is doing the same. Counselling is becoming a work-place strategy which has the interest of the counsellor at heart and not necessarily those of the clients. The role of the qualification in counselling is exclusion rather than testing professional competence. You could have a very competent counsellor who is competent on the basis of their qualities but that would allow any number of people to become counsellors, which would disrupt the professional aspirations of a lot of counsellors.

One respondent discussed the use of counselling in terms of its *structure* and how little or much the counselling relationship needed to be structured.

> It can be used on a daily basis or on an informal basis with contacts with colleagues and people you are attached to. I guess this is the more informal type of counselling. Then there are the more professional settings – tutors to students for example, when you have to make yourself approachable to the students. That needs a little bit more thought. Some of the people who are tutors are therefore academic tutoring, others are there for all aspects of the student's life. Perhaps a middle path is necessary here: where tutors are prepared to listen to what is going on outside the student's immediate academic arena.

Another talked of 'formalised' counselling (as opposed, presumably, to informal or 'friendly' counselling). He noted, too, some possible *arenas* for counselling.

> There is the more highly formalised counselling situation – counselling people, getting paid to do it, perhaps being part of a team helping GPs, psychiatrists etc. You may be a practitioner in a psychiatric unit or other care setting. All of these different situations are ones in which some form of counselling might be called for.

Another respondent made this distinction between 'formal' and 'informal' approaches to counselling more explicit:

> There are at least two types of counselling: the informal, ordinary, unspectacular way of helping and the more professional side of things. I find that the phoniness you meet sometimes – the tilted head, the voice changing – may be a result of the training. I find that off-putting. What I need when I discuss something with somebody else is a gut reaction – a more spontaneous reaction. I would not approach a stranger for that. I would need to know the person was genuinely interested in me.

Yet another respondent talked of the difficulty of training counsellors and of the paradox between 'being spontaneous' and 'being a professional':

The spontaneous part of counselling is very very difficult to train at all. It has to do with people knowing their limitations and their likes and dislikes. As you professionalise something there is the tendency to make things more special, more detached from the real side of a relationship. Something gets lost. There is a risk of losing the spontaneous side of the interaction.

Others saw the value of counselling as lying within the process of helping people to become more responsible for themselves and re-exercising some control over what happens to them:

It can be used to enable people to examine specific problems or life situations which they would like resolved or changed. To enable them to make the best use of resources, to examine relationships, to make choices, to discover the choices available to them. To help them become more responsible for themselves and to use that responsibility over their own lives. To enable them to feel more in control of their situation. To enable them to be in a relationship with a counsellor which will enable them to develop learning about themselves. And to make those discoveries in a situation which, although it may be uncomfortable, is safe.

It can be used to enable people to problem-solve, to identify sources of discomfort or stress and it can be used to alleviate problems of living – everyday problems of living such as anxiety and general feelings that people have of being 'outside'. It can also enhance basic communication. It can also be used, perhaps, inappropriately. It can be used as a disguise for basic disciplinary measures and it can be hijacked to disguise commercial activities such as beauty counsellors, financial counsellors etc.

Some respondents felt there was a tension between health-care professionals offering counselling and counselling being viewed as a 'treatment'. It was seen as essential that becoming involved in counselling should be a voluntary activity on the part of the patient or client.

I don't think there is ever a 'should' – 'this person should see a counsellor'. If they are not ready and they don't want it, then there is no point. I very much believe in people's rights to live their own life the way they want and not have counselling. When somebody is going through a traumatic experience then there are all sorts of problems that are unresolved particularly when they do not have other people in their lives to talk to. Even when people do have lots of other people counselling is quite different. Family and friends will not talk to you in the same way. Counsellors are impartial and will not necessarily just go with you. Friends will not want to upset you whereas counselling can be more penetrating and challenging – which friends will not always be – unless they are special friends. Any sorts of problems – mid-life crises 'what's it all about' – those sorts of issues can be addressed in counselling.

When counselling should not be used

Respondents talked about when counselling *should not* be used – contraindications of counselling. These were wide ranging and are reported below. The first seems to relate to the misuse of certain sorts of training procedures.

> It shouldn't be used as a habit or for recreational purposes. I have seen some people who seem to be addicted to it. It becomes a substitution for normal human intercourse and sometimes people's motives are poor for going into it in the first place – such as group counselling as a place to pick up women.

> There may be a danger that a vulnerable person could be exposed psychologically or abused – using the term broadly. If you were, for example, attracted to a person of the opposite sex, or the same sex, that may infect the situation if you had a lot of contact with them. As a counsellor you need to be pretty solid, you need to know what you are doing and your integrity is not going to be called into question. You have to be seen as being detached but that's not a word that rests easy, you have to be comfortable in your own skin – whatever people say to you, you're not going to be tempted to abuse the relationship. Those things relate more to the professional dimension than to the ordinary side.

Sometimes, the issue was an ideological one. It was noted by one respondent that the prevailing philosophy in counselling is the 'client-centred' one in which the client is *always* encouraged to find his or her own solutions to his or her problems and in which direct, prescriptive intervention on the part of the client is usually eschewed.

It may depend on the type of counselling the counsellor wishes to adopt. To adopt a non-directive approach with people, where it is patently obvious that you should be making suggestions, is very wasteful, I think there are lots of people who seek out help who want a direction and to keep throwing back on them and ask them to make every decision is sometimes inappropriate. People are pretty good at problem-solving and are likely to respond much better to the non-directive approach but there are people who find it difficult to make any decisions and then it is appropriate to make more concrete suggestions as to what they may do.

Sometimes, the fact that counselling was not a panacea was noted and it was made clear that counselling had very definite limitations. The following respondents highlight the problems of the then current practice of counsellors being 'to hand' after a major disaster.

There may be situations where the problem cannot be solved in your head – and I'm thinking about lack of money, serious illness, unemployment – those sorts of things. Counselling may help but some of those very serious problems aren't ones that can be solved. On these emergency situations that we see on the TV – kids drowning, accidents and things – it's amazing how quickly counselling services are set up. And yet what most normal people would be is in a state of shock at that time, and its seems likely that only afterwards people need counselling – not immediately afterwards. I can't see how anyone can sit in an aircraft hanger and have twenty counsellors dashing towards them. You have the same sort of situation when children have been murdered or have disappeared and you have loads of counsellors dashing round to the school to these thirteen or fourteen year olds to do counselling, when all they need probably is to be reassured by their parents.

I think I would also agree with those who feel that the presence of counsellors at disasters is probably inappropriate. You get a vision of 'therapeutic vultures' perhaps when people are in extreme distress they need time to be distressed. Because counselling is not a universal panacea for the human condition.

Sometimes, the client-centred approach, referred to above, was seen as limited and one respondent called for a much wider approach to be used.

When the counsellor has other motives other than to help the client: when the counsellor is in a situation which he himself ought to take responsibility for the situation, either because of former responsibilities for it or when not to do so would cause undue pain to the client – such as when you get situations in which people steadfastly avoid giving advice by trying to be Rogerian – when the best thing would be to tell the person what to do. I recognise that in counselling you would tend to avoid that but sometimes it would be more appropriate.

The question of the counsellor's 'detachment' was another issue that was discussed by some of the respondents. In this context the issue of 'boundaries' was also discussed.

I think that where there is another relationship in which it is impossible for the counsellor to be detached – as opposed to relatives, that sort of thing. That is not to imply you can never help people close to you because I think you can. It's just that there's a way of being in counselling which is not appropriate to close relationships, family or sex relationships. I think it is about boundaries in counselling so that it would be inappropriate for me to take on a student for counselling in its pure sense where I also had another relationship where I also judged the student. That is not to say that I cannot help the students but that I would not take them on for a review of their personal life situation and would recommend that they get their help from someone else.

There are real problems when the client doesn't want counselling. In fact when the individual does not want to be a client. This is a particular problem of people on counselling courses who insist on asking people 'how they feel'. It should not be used as a crowbar for intruding into people's privacy.

The advantages of counselling

Various advantages of counselling were identified by the respondents. One respondent identified its *economic* advantages. He also referred, in passing, to the role of the Church in counselling and the idea of 'counselling as a replacement for a priest'.

It can help you over an immediate crisis or problem. If you are upset you often can't see a way out of a predicament. It's a cheap relative to psychoanalysis or psychotherapy. It is also widely available. A counsellor will give you time in a way that a doctor won't. And for an atheist like myself, a priest is not really an alternative. For a religious person, a priest may be the most appropriate person as the problem may have a spiritual content.

Others found other advantages but often these were *qualified* in various ways suggesting that with the various advantages also came other disadvantages.

My guess is that it helps people just to get on with their lives. The fact is that I think lots of people can do it. But it does need a willingness and a genuine interest in other human beings which is difficult to 'manufacture'. It can be pretty cheap – a cheap way of helping people. The less formal types of counselling perhaps allow the person who needs the help to maintain some dignity and integrity in the whole process and it's not like going to your doctor or going to a psychiatrist because your whole life is falling apart – it's sort of more acceptable to society. You can say to people 'I'm going for some counselling' but it is more difficult to say 'I was mentally ill'. There is a greater willingness for people to take counselling on board as acceptable.

[Counselling helps people to have] the opportunity to have a safe situation in which one explores options and choices – particularly where some of those choices may be frightening or where some disclosures of some aspects of one's self may be a presentation of self that one wouldn't want seen elsewhere. If I am looking at a side of myself that I don't want to show to people in everyday life but I need to understand, then I may need the confidentiality of a counselling relationship in order to do that.

Sometimes, the view was taken that 'counselling works because people say that it does'.

For the client it would seem to help. I am not sure why. Perhaps I am a bit but it seems to help. I've seen it help. And sometimes afterwards I've wondered what I've done that I valued so much and that I missed. I guess that relates to the intuitive nature of counselling if you have counselled for a while.

The disadvantages of counselling

There were also clearly identified *disadvantages* to counselling. Again, these were quite wide-ranging.

> It can mislead people into thinking it's a solution, when in fact a real solution may be a material change in the person's circumstances which the counsellor can do nothing to effect. There are a lot of charlatans in counselling. When there is money changing hands the counsellors may have more interest in prolonging the sessions. It is a straightforward market relation sometimes. And like all market relations the profit is a motive and not a human need. The other thing is it is just another way of accommodating oneself to what may be a horrible situation and a better response may be a political one.

One respondent had doubts about the purported practice of teaching student health-care professionals counselling skills as part of their training, arguing that counsellors needed some maturity and some life experience in order to both help the client and to take care of themselves:

> One of the things which is true about counselling is that is has become reified – it has become elevated to a supernatural status – particularly in nursing. So much so that every curriculum document must have an element of counselling in it. My feeling is that many of the students that I have dealt with are anywhere between 17 and 22 and I do believe that if you're going to be a good counsellor you need to have more life experience as it will help you to put things in perspective. It seems that some courses are expecting to put these young people into counselling and turn them out as mini-counsellors in any arena. I don't think that this is realistic and this is one of the problems as the thing has become more popular. So you have people coming out of courses who will I think have done all these hours of counselling training but these are not underpinned by the years of experience that are needed to be a good counsellor.

Other disadvantages were also noted.

> There is the potential opportunity to abuse other people's vulnerability. People do enjoy having power, as experts over people who

are very vulnerable and I think this is something to have to guard against.

I would want to distinguish between bad counselling – which one could find quite easily and which could be disempowering and could produce dependency, could mean the person does not own their own decisions. I think there is a continuum in counselling. As counselling gets better the likelihood of this happening is reduced.

For the client perhaps, they may feel that it doesn't supply them with any answers. The process can be seen as rather slow or even traumatic.

For the counsellor the disadvantages are that it opens you to an awareness of another person's pain that you may have to avoid due to the situation you are in. And perhaps it can make you weary of other people's distress.

These interviews give examples of the ways in which practising counsellors or helpers and trainers feel about one aspect of the inter-personal skills field. Many of the features of effective counselling – the ability to listen, the ability to focus your attention on the *other person's* problem and so on – are all related to a more general interpersonal skill – that of being able to relate to people in a therapeutic way.

Types of counselling

Counselling as information seeking

This is perhaps the most straightforward type of counselling and helping. Here, a person approaches a counsellor or helper to find out specific information. An example would be the person who requires information about safe sex in relation to the prevention of the spread of the HIV virus. Clearly, anyone who engages in information giving needs to be certain that the information they are giving out is accurate and up to date. This is clearly a case of 'if you don't know, don't make it up'. For some, there is a temptation to want to be seen as an expert and never to be 'wrong'. There is a great danger attached to this posi-tion in that faulty or wrong information can clearly misguide the enquirer. Also, because the helper has been identified as some sort of expert, the chances are that the enquirer will act on the information given.

A distinction can be made between information giving and advice giving. The former is the passing on of things that are known. The latter is the passing on of what the helper *thinks* is an appropriate way to act. It might be suggested that it would be better for most of us to stick to offering the former than the latter. The exception to this is when we are expert in a particular field and can offer advice that sits alongside information. For instance, a lawyer or solicitor has a certain knowledge about a range of legal issues and offers information and can also offer an informed view on what *might* be done. Advice given, then, might best be restricted to concrete situations in which it is linked to specific information. It seems to me that it is often less than useful to offer other people advice about 'how to run their lives'. We may be experts in our own lives (although often this is not the case): we are certainly not experts in other people's lives.

Counselling as confession

Sometimes helpers take over the role traditionally occupied, perhaps, by the clergy: they listen to people who need to share incidents in their lives that are difficult to talk about. They need, in a way, to 'confess'. It is worth considering what happens when this takes place. Although there is no sense in which a helper can offer any sort of absolution he or she may be viewed as someone who 'forgives' the other person. In listening to what is difficult for the other person to talk about, the helper is also, in some ways, taking on a certain responsibility for the other person. Once something has been said, it cannot be unsaid. Similarly, once we have heard something, once someone has told us something, we cannot 'not know' that fact about them. To disclose to another person, then, is to ask them to take a certain responsibility for us.

This, in turn, raises a moral question and a serious one. We have to consider the degree to which we can offer complete confidentiality in the helping relationship. There is, I believe, a fairly straightforward answer to the confidentiality issue. As a rule, and except in life-or-death situations, we probably cannot guarantee confidentiality to another person, in advance of what they have to say. For the fact is that we cannot *know* what it is they are going to tell us. If, for example, a person asks for our complete confidence and then tells us that they are going to commit suicide, we would be acting in a very debatable way if we were to continue to offer complete confidentiality. There are, of course, organisations such as the Samaritans, in the UK, who *do* offer complete confidentiality. But it is also true that such people work as teams and are able to draw on each other's experience and support when faced with very difficult situations.

Perhaps a safer way of working with others is to offer confidentiality on a 'need to know' basis. That is to say that I will keep what you tell me in confidence unless what you tell me leads to a situation that neither you nor I can adequately handle. The example of the person threatening suicide is one example where it would be reasonable to break confidence. Another example would be when a person says that he or she intends to commit serious assault on another person. Again, it would be reasonable to break confidence in a situation like this. This form of 'limited confidentiality' is essential in the helping professions such as nursing and medicine where such professionals are bound by codes of ethics to ensure that they do not allow others to do themselves (or others) harm.

At this point, the question may be raised whether you can *refuse* confidentiality to another person. Surely, if a person really wants to talk to you in confidence, then they are not going to talk to you if that confidence is denied. While this may occasionally happen, experience indicates that people who really need to talk are likely to do so whether that talking is in complete confidence. That is not to say that people will talk to other people who share everything they say with others but to note that a person comes to you, usually, because he or she *trusts* you. The idea that you will not, automatically, pass on what he or she says, becomes a given. Within the idea of trust is also the idea that you will maintain confidentiality on those matters that another person does not want you to share and which are not of such magnitude that sharing with others is essential. However, the rule remains that, in extreme situations, confidentiality is likely to have to be broken.

Counselling as problem solving

People with problems often seek out another person as a sounding board: someone with whom they can talk over their problems, experiment with various solutions and finally reach some resolution. Examples of this approach are seen when people have relationship difficulties or want to change jobs or where they live. There are various views about how people should be helped in the problem-solving process. At one extreme, the counsellor or helper is seen as someone who stays in the background, who facilitates the other person's identifying their own problems and their own solutions to those problems. At the other extreme, the counsellor may be a person who has very particular experience and who can *offer* suggestions as to how problems might be solved. The traditional approach to counselling eschews the latter approach: it is argued that *only* the person with problems can identify his or her difficulties and find ways of working through them. To me, though, this sometimes involves a degree of reinventing the wheel. Many of us have been through life situations that, although not identical to those of others, are similar. It seems to me that, sometimes, it can be appropriate to make suggestions as to how another person my find their way out of a life problem. This may be particularly true where concrete life situations are involved. The person, for example, who wants to change his or her job may be advised by another person who has experience of the job opportunities and job structures that exist in related careers. Similarly, the person who is worried about moving to work in another country might well be helped by the person who knows a considerable amount about that country. It should not, in my view, be taken for granted that advice is *always* inappropriate in counselling.

On the other hand, there is a line to be drawn between helping another person by offering suggestions and taking over the other person's problems. If we offer too much advice and become too prescriptive we risk the other person becoming dependent on us. We also set ourselves up, unreasonably, as a scapegoat if things go wrong. If we advise and the advice turns out not to be appropriate, then the person who talked to us about their problems is likely to resent us for giving them what is perceived as bad advice.

Counselling as befriending

Many of us who are fortunate to have a variety of friends often use those friends to talk through anxieties and worries. In that sense, we use them as counsellors – albeit informal ones. For the person who, for whatever reason, has few or no friends, the counsellor can take the place of a friend. He or she can stand alongside the other person and offer support and encouragement. The question that can be raised, here, or course, is to what degree can someone be a 'professional' friend? Is it possible for a health-care worker, a volunteer or a care-line helper to act as a true friend to someone who comes to them for help? The question must remain an open one and one for further debate. Mostly, presumably, we choose our friends or friendship occurs, spontaneously, over time. In the counselling and helping relationship, roles are quite clearly prescribed: one person is the counsellor or helper and the other is a client, patient or whatever else the 'helpee' is called. In more regular, everyday friendships, there is not this demarcation between the helping and the helped. In ordinary friendships, the roles fluctuate with – at times – one person taking the role of the helper and – at times – the other taking on this role.

The metaphor of the counsellor as friend, though, is an attractive one in that it seems to blur the boundaries between one person being a professional and the other being someone in need. In theory, at least, it appears to merge those boundaries and make the relationship equal. Perhaps, in the end, it is possible for the two people involved to move towards such an equal relationship: one in which the usual fluctuations of helping and being helped become possible. Much will depend, perhaps, on the counsellor's need or belief in the need to stay 'separate' from the person being helped.

This debate, in turn, leads to one about whether counsellors and their clients should remain 'friends' over time. Some would see the counselling relationship as time-bound in some way while others may see it as quite possible to continue to know the other person after acute problems have passed.

Counselling as catharsis

Catharsis, in this context, is the release of strong emotion – usually through tears or expression of anger. Some people find it difficult to express these sorts of feelings with people to whom they are close and find the counselling relationship one in which such release is possible. There are mixed views about the value of such emotional release. Those who subscribe to the psychodynamic or humanistic approaches to counselling often view catharsis as an important, if not vital, part of the counselling process. Others, however, see it is a means of 'learning how to express more emotion'. In the latter case, the view is taken that tears simply lead to the expression of more tears and are not, in themselves, healing in any way.

I suspect that no fixed rules can be laid down here. It is probable that many people find the occasional (or even frequent) release of emotion helpful. It is also probable that other people find it more helpful to consider problems in a cooler fashion and prefer a rational approach to dealing with difficulties. As always, there is a danger that the counsellor or helper will take his or her own way of dealing with problems as *the* way or, alternatively, he or she will adopt a particular theoretical position (in this case, one related to catharsis) and believe that it *always* applies. It seems to me that given that people vary considerably on all sorts of dimensions, they also vary on this one: catharsis helps some people and not others.

The other issue that arises here is what to do if someone *does* express strong emotion. Much will depend on a range of issues: the counsellor's own experience of emotional release; his or her competence in helping others in emotional distress and so on. These issues will be discussed, in more detail, later in this book.

Counselling as debate

Sometimes, what a person with problems needs is someone with whom to debate the issues. Often, we carry out this sort of exercise in our own heads: we weigh up the pros and cons of a situation, worry at them, until we reach a decision. At other times, it is useful to have another person to act either as a facilitator or as someone prepared to argue with us, to put the other side of the story. The problem with debate with ourselves is that we only have a very particular set of points of view – the ones we can think up ourselves. Having a counsellor or helper acting as part of the debate can raise other possibilities.

The counsellor or helper who acts in this capacity may play devil's advocate to the other person. He or she may raise objections, spot flaws in an argument or identify other ways of seeing or doing things. Such a counsellor may also check with the other person the appropriateness of a course of action by asking such questions as: 'what might happen if you do that?', 'what is the likely outcome of that approach? or 'what will happen if you *don't* do that?'

It seems to me that there is a place, in certain circumstances, for fairly heated debate and even argument between the counsellor and the person he or she is trying to help. Again, this sort of situation frequently arises amongst friends and it is often through active conflict over an issue that we finally reach resolution. Here, the sorts of interventions that the counsellor or helper may use include such questions as 'what evidence do you have for thinking that way?' or 'can you give me some more examples of how that is the case?' Clearly, the counsellor is not seeking to be antagonistic for its own sake but is confronting the other person on some of their more restricted and restrictive ways of thinking. Many of us tend to think along 'tramlines' – we get set in our ways of thinking about problems. The counsellor who challenges can help the other person towards fresh ways of thinking about old problems.

Counselling as support

This approach is almost the opposite of the one described in the last few paragraphs. Here, the aim is to offer a person who is clearly suffering in some way, an arm to lean on. Counselling as support is a method of helping another person to cope with a possibly over-whelming set of circumstances. Examples of where such support is likely to be needed are after a bereavement, during serious illness or following the breakdown of a close relationship. Such situations do not require debate and confrontation but simply the supportive presence of another person who is prepared to listen and to help 'contain' the other person's distress.

An issue that frequently occurs in the debate about support is whether the counsellor or helper needs to have been through similar experiences to the person they are supporting in order to help them. For example, is a bereaved counsellor the best person to help another bereaved person? Do you have to have lived through relationship break-down yourself in order to support another person through such a crisis. The debate breaks down into at least two paths. On the one hand, the person who has had similar experiences to the person to whom he or she is talking obviously 'knows' something of the experience of that person. On the other hand, it can also be argued that a person who has been through a similar situation may be too 'close' to the problem and likely to act as if he or she has been through *exactly* the same situation as the person being helped. In the end, it seems unlikely that we can make too many generalisations about how different people experience life events. How *I* experience bereavement and serious illness may be quite different to the way that *you* do. By extension, it may be wrong of me to assume that because I have been bereaved I am in a 'better' position to help others in similar circumstances.

At the other end of the scale, however, it also seems unlikely that a person with very little life experience is going to be fully equipped to help others deal with serious personal problems. And perhaps it is here that we can find some resolution to this apparent dilemma. What may count, in the end, is that the person who is offering support has both a wide range of life experiences but also the capacity to lay his or her experiences to one side as he or she listens to the other person's distress. Arguably, the fact of having a range of difficult life situations yourself allows you to realise that there are no easy answers to them in other people's lives.

Nor, perhaps, should support take the form of glib reassurance. None of us can predict how a person's problems may work out (or not work out) in the end. Simply to attempt to assure someone that 'everything will work out in the end' is unlikely to be seen as support. The idea of support, in counselling, often involves the notion of being able to 'hold' or 'contain' the other person as they experience their distress. In this sense, the counsellor becomes a person onto whom the distressed person can cling for a period until they find their capacity to cope independently.

Counselling as a form of personal growth

A more contentious area in the field is that of counselling as a form of personal growth. Some see value in working with a counsellor in order to find out more about themselves and thus to 'grow'. However, the metaphor of growth, in terms of human beings, is far from clear. Humanistic psychologists sometimes argue that we all have 'hidden potential' that can, in various ways and in various circumstances, be tapped. Others see life as offering the possibility of working towards our full capacity as human beings. However, another view is that we are constantly working on the human project: that we cannot anticipate, in advance, the direction in which we will develop as human beings. In this case, it is impossible to know, with any certainty, whether or not we will 'grow' in this way. Nor, perhaps, is such growth a constant. It seems likely that many people's lives are a sequence of peaks and troughs, of 'growth' and 'consolidation'. However, for the person who either likes the idea of 'working on themselves' or who lives an anxious and troubled life, without being frankly ill, such counselling can be helpful.

There is also considerable discussion about whether those who work as counsellors and helpers should, themselves, be counselled. This is a case, perhaps, of 'physician heal thyself'. Whether or not any given counsellor subscribes to the notion of being in on-going counselling themselves, it does seem likely that the person who is very troubled in their own lives is unlikely to be able to offer others the sustained support and help that is required of a person acting as a counsellor. If we are too caught up in our own difficulties, we are likely to find that the person to whom we are offering counselling sparks off too many problems in our own heads. Then, we find it difficult to draw the line between what constitutes our own problems and those of the person we are counselling.

It may even be possible that some people are drawn to counselling (as practitioners) in order to try to come to terms with their own problems – as a means of some sort of reassurance that 'other people's problems are far worse than mine'. This does not, however, seem to be a good basis from which to work. Ideally, perhaps, the counsellor should be a person who, while not having resolved all their own problems, is at least aware of many of them and able to live reasonably comfortably with them.

Distinguishing between counselling and helping

It is at this point that it may be useful to make a distinction between counselling and helping. As we have seen, there are various forms of counselling, various people can do it and it can be used in a variety of ways. Trying to search for the ultimate definition of exactly what counselling *is* may prove to be impossible. Instead, I want to suggest that using the word *helping* as a general approach to working with people may be more useful for many people. Although 'helping' is an even broader concept than counselling, it has the big advantage of not carrying around with it the 'baggage' that has become attached to counselling. Few people, presumably, mind being helped, whereas some may not wish to submit themselves to counselling. So, although I occasionally use the term 'counselling' in the rest of the book, I am generally happier with the term 'helping'. The term is meant to indicate that *anyone* who works with other people is likely to be able to act in a helping capacity. It is also assumed that the type of helping being offered, in this context, is that which involves talking about problems, seeking solutions, befriending and so on. What is *not* assumed is that the helper necessarily has to work from a particular theoretical base. Helping does not automatically suggest that the helper brings a particular psychological slant to his or her work. In essence, then, we can *all* help other people, even if we are not all trained as counsellors.

2   Why counsel or help?

In this chapter I address the question: *'why should people help?'*
Already, the ground is thorny. The question, itself, begs previous questions. Can we assume that people *do* help, as a matter of course? Is
helping *necessarily* part of a person's role? Are we clear enough about
the *nature* of helping to prescribe it as part of that role? For the
purposes of this chapter, we must take it as read that helping *is* part of
the person's role but that what needs further debate is the *why* of the
issue. This will not necessarily be a comfortable debate and, as with
any 'abstract' debates, more questions will be asked than can ever be
answered. If, however, we want to consider ourselves as counsellors
and helpers, it is a question that needs to be addressed.

It would seem that the debate opens up in at least three directions.
There would seem to be *contractual, ethical* and *spiritual* issues
involved. In this chapter, all three will be addressed although greater
emphasis will be given to the last two. The contractual issues would
seem to be the easiest ones with which to deal.

Contractual issues

In answer to the question *why should people help?* we may want to
answer *because some are under contractual obligation to do so.* We may
argue, for instance, that the business of being a health-care professional, pastoral or voluntary worker involves the notion of helping and
that to offer clients a service, at all, is to offer them helping. Not to
offer them helping, on the other hand, is not to offer them a service. In
this sense, what we do as health-care professionals or voluntary workers
is *defined* in relation to helping. A parallel may be with *teaching* and
learning. It would be odd to argue (as is sometimes the case) that a
teacher has *taught* a topic but that no learning took place. To engage in
teaching is to engage in the process of ensuring that learning is occur-

ring. If a teacher really has taught something, then students really have learned. If learning has *not* taken place, then a subject has not been taught.

Similarly, we might want to say that if a person is engaged in working with others, then they will have *helped*. If they have not helped, then they have been engaged in something but that 'something' is not 'working with others'. To work with others, then, in health care and related fields, is to help.

At a more concrete level, it might be argued that help is offered on the basis of patient or client expectation. We might say that the patient or client *expects* help from a person as part of the contract that they have entered into. To be a patient or client, in this case, is to expect help and to be a person, in this case, is to offer that help. Similarly, it might be proposed that people are *employed* to offer help. Here, the nature of the contract between people and employees is based on an expectation that the people will offer help. It needs to be said, though, that such a contractual issue is more an *implicit* than explicit one. It seems likely that very few formal contracts will include 'help clauses' – at least in the short term. It seems possible that, in the future, helping *may* be formalised in this way – and this opens up further problems.

If helping *is* a contractual issue, we need to consider the implications of this. There may be an apparent contradiction of the fact that health professions are called upon to help but are also *paid* to do so. It is as though the counsellor or helper is being called upon to 'turn on' their help, according to their financial contract. This state of affairs is similar to that found in helping and psychotherapy in which the client pays a professional person to sympathise, empathise and listen. The open question remains: can a person help *professionally* and for money?

The sort of debate that usually occurs at this point is whether a paid helper is 'genuine'. The argument seems to revolve around the idea that genuineness is somehow a 'natural' state of affairs whereas the introduction of a profit motive brings an unnaturalness to the proceedings. This sort of argument often surfaces when people discuss the naturalness or otherwise of cabin crew in aircraft, hotel and restaurant staff and even service staff in McDonald's! A view is often expressed that if people have to be *trained* in working with the public, then they are likely to be 'artificial' or 'unnatural'. Sometimes, this sort of argument is even levelled at a whole country or culture as is seen in the statement that 'Americans are shallow and insincere'. This sort of sentiment is often based on the high levels of attention paid to greeting and thanking that occurs in American service industries. The phrase 'have a nice day' has, for the British, become synonymous with insincerity.

There is, however, another way of looking at all this. The argument may be levelled that we have *all* 'learned' to relate to others. If we help, we do so because we have *learned* to help. That learning process may have occurred over a number of years. It might be argued, for example, that we learned to help by being helped – by parents, friends, lovers and partners. We have experienced help and therefore are able to show help in return. We may also have learned to help vicariously – by observing other people being helped. All of this amounts to a learning process.

If we return to the debate about professional helpers, we may find that cabin crew, hotel staff and so on have also *learned* to help – but have done so in a highly structured, intentional way. The process has been speeded up and although the *methods of learning* may be different, it can still be argued that such staff have learned to help. So it may be with people. There is no reason why we should automatically assume that helping 'comes naturally' to some people, nor even that it must always be spontaneous and straight from the heart. There need be nothing particularly sinister about the person who sets out to improve her or his helping skills or who plans to help another person. We train counsellors and psychotherapists. There seems no reason to assume that we should not, also, train helpers. If we can decide upon what constitutes a helping disposition or attitude, then we may be able to isolate the elements that need to be taught in a 'helping syllabus'. Just now, those elements have *not* been identified particularly clearly but there is no reason to assume that future research will not isolate them. Nor need this become a debate over holism versus reductionism. We can analyse the concept of helping – as a means of helping to teach it – without dissecting the *person*. The person remains a 'whole' even if, for training purposes, we filter out some elements of our relationship with that person.

Looked at from a social contract point of view, interpersonal life may be viewed as a series of transactions in which each person does things for and with another person in anticipation of receiving something. This is a day-to-day example of the general rule that 'there is no such thing as a free lunch'. In this context, it means that people help in order to get something in return. They help so that they will be thanked or rewarded in less tangible ways. What reinforces their helping behaviour is the fact of that reward. In this model, no one does things out of empathy or true compassion for others but because there will always be a pay-off. A less cynical view might be that we help *because* we are paid. The 'return', in this case, is payment itself. Either way, the issue of helping is, again, a contractual one. People are employed to be helping and are paid because they help.

There is yet another, more human, aspect to the contractual debate. Martin Buber (1958) in a complex essay on interpersonal relations compared and contrasted the 'I–It' relationship with the 'I–Thou' relationship. These ideas have slipped into many papers and discussions about the nature of helping. In essence, Buber's argument was this: that when we deal with people on an 'I–It' basis, we turn them into objects. This sort of objectification can be seen when members of the medical and nursing professions refer to other people as 'the appendix in bed six'. Suddenly, the breathing, feeling, living person has become 'an appendix' – an object. Buber argues that a more human – and more morally defensible position – is to treat people from the point of view of an 'I–Thou' relationship. In such a relationship, each person meets the other as a conscious, knowing and feeling human being. In meeting you as a 'thou', I respect your humanity. (It should be noted, at this point, that the 'thou' issue is something of a problem in the English language. In the French and German languages – to name but two – 'thou' is the 'familiar' version of addressing another person. In the English language, no distinction is made between a 'personal' address and a more 'formal' address and this makes the discussion of the I–Thou issue a little more complicated because these distinctions are lost.)

What Buber is addressing is another version of the contractual issue (although it shades over into the domain of ethics). He is arguing that part of the process of working with other human beings is to acknowledge *their* humanness. Part of the 'contract' of being a helper or a therapist is *not* to turn them into an object but to allow them to remain people and people on equal terms with ourselves. To do this involves constant vigilance and a great deal of humility. For if we are to retain the 'I–Thou' mode of relations, we must forgo any 'professional' pretensions that we may have. For to treat people from a professional point of view might involve turning them into objects.

These, then, are aspects of the contractual approach to helping. From this point of view, person–patient relationships are seen as variously defined and negotiated relationships that involve some sort of reciprocity between the two parties. In such relationships, each party is seen as having some sort of need that requires fulfilment. Helping, from this point of view, is as much about the fulfilment of various needs as it is an innate human condition.

Ethical issues

Another approach to the question of 'why help?' is an ethical one. Ethical questions are one of right or wrong, of how to make appropriate decisions, of how to act in a given situation. In this case, we may ask 'on what grounds is it appropriate for me, as a person, to act in a helping way?'

There are various ways of approaching ethical issues. One, for example, is through appeal to a religious code of some sort that instructs the believer in ways to act. As spiritual issues are discussed later in this chapter, these approaches to solving ethical dilemmas are not addressed here – except to note that most religious codes implore believers to act helpingly towards other people. We might even be tempted to argue that a religious person is usually duty bound to act in a helping way towards other people. Ironically, however, even the briefest of glances at the world picture will reveal that religion is also behind many of the international instances of people *not* helping each other. And therein lies an almost imponderable paradox: that whilst – as far as we can tell – all religions insist on the helping treatment of others, most are also a potential source of very unhelping behaviour.

We need, then, to turn to secular approaches to the ethics of helping. By secular, I mean, here, those approaches that do not, necessarily, draw on religious codes of behaviour – although the two are often compatible. There is no reason to suppose that a secular approach to ethics automatically rules out a particular religious code.

A widely cited source of guidance in ethical matters is Kant's injunction that we should act as though our behaviour was illustrating a universal law of behaviour. In other words, when we act, we must do so believing that the behaviour would be one that *anyone* might reasonably engage in. A right action, then, is one that is *universally* right. This is the basis of Kant's *categorical imperative*.

Using this position, it might thus be possible to argue that the reason we *should* help is that we would hope to be helped ourselves. We would also hope that help would be extended to all the people that we know and love. In this way, helping is almost a necessary human behaviour because *absence* of help is, similarly, unacceptable as a universal principle. If I say, for example, that it does not matter if I help or not, I am (according to the principles so far outlined) arguing that it matters not if *anyone* helps. Presumably, I would not want to live in a world in which no-one helps others and so helping becomes an imperative. Nor does a middle position seem tenable. Presumably, I would find it difficult to argue that it could be a universal principle that people should be 'indifferent' to each other – neither helping nor not helping. It might even be mooted that such indifference was *worse* than not helping. The evidence – if it can be called that – from the Kantian principle, seems to be that helping is a necessary human act and one that I am compelled to offer because I, too, am human. To act in less than a helping way is to *justify* a lack of helping.

Another approach to considering ethical issues is Mill's *utilitarianism* – an approach first articulated by Jeremy Bentham. Utilitarianism is often summed up by the slogan that 'that which is good is that which causes the greatest happiness to the greatest number' or slight variants of it. It seems reasonable to argue that helping is *unlikely* to cause widespread unhappiness and, therefore, can be justified as a 'good' action. Put in a positive version, it seems possible to say that it is likely that helping *will* cause fairly widespread happiness and can, again, be justified. All this, of course, hangs on how 'helping' might be defined and this, again, is debated throughout this volume. It would seem difficult, however, to argue that helping was *not* a 'positive' concept. Whatever helping is *not* it seems likely that it can be always be defined in positive, life-enhancing ways.

Yet another approach to ethics is by way of *existentialism*. Existentialism is a particular and distinctive approach to philosophy. It cannot really be described as a 'school' of philosophy as it is, by its nature, anti-systems-building and may even be described as anarchical in its approach. Perhaps the most populist definition of existentialism as an approach to philosophy was offered by Jean-Paul Sartre in his 1949 essay *Existentialism is a Humanism* (usually translated as *Existentialism and Humanism*) (Sartre 1952). Sartre sums up the heart of existentialism through the slogan 'existence predates essence' and, given existentialism's influence on counselling theory and on patient-centred approaches to help, it may be worth considering it in a little more detail.

What does it mean to say that *existence predates essence*? First, it is often useful to consider the *opposite* of what it means and the example that Sartre employs is useful. He asks the reader to consider a paper knife. Before a paper knife comes into existence, its form and function (or its *essence*) has already been determined. Someone has sat down and given thought to what other people might need to use to open letters. That person has then designed the implement and other people have worked on manufacturing it. Once the paper knife comes into existence, its 'essence' has largely been fixed.

Sartre argues that, for human beings, exactly the opposite is the case. There is no blueprint for the person. He or she is simply 'thrown into the world' (to borrow an expression from Heidegger). The existential position, then, is this: that a person 'comes into existence' and that person's 'essence' or 'personhood' only emerges later. And this essence (and this is a vital point) is whatever that person makes it. He or she is the 'author of his or her essence'. For Sartre, a person is both free and responsible. He or she is free to become whatever he or she makes of himself or herself. Because of that freedom, the person is also *responsible* for what he or she becomes. We cannot be free and *not* responsible. Consider, for example, if I make the statement 'I am free to do what I want, but I must check things, first, with my wife'! Clearly, I am not free. I can *only* be free if I acknowledge that there is no one else that can choose for me. If I am free, I am free to make decisions and those decisions *always* involve the exercise of responsibility. Sartre writes of the 'anguish' of choice. Choosing for oneself is difficult on a number of counts. First, I *must* choose. Even *not* choosing involves a form of 'negative choice'. Second, no one, in the end, can make decisions for me: I am on my own. Third, no one can really *advise* me. They have not had my life experiences and cannot take responsibility for the outcome of my life decisions.

If all of this is true for all individuals, it raises questions about how I *should* choose. What rules are there to guide me? Sartre's answer to this is fairly terse and along the lines of 'there are none!' Choice and decision making, for Sartre, are necessarily lonely and idiosyncratic actions. However, he acknowledges that *everyone* is in this position. I am not choosing in isolation. I am surrounded, also, by a wide range of 'others' who are also choosing. Thus, when I *do* choose, I nearly always find myself taking into account the effects of those choices on those around me (after all, as we have noted, I carry the responsibility for those choices). Each choice I make is likely to have some sort of impact on other people. Consider, for example, if – as a married person with children – I decide to leave this country and go and live in splendid isolation on a distant island. Clearly, the responsibility for such an action is mine. Only I can decide to do this. However, I must also consider the *responsibility* that goes with such an action. Like it or not, other people will be affected by my action: my wife, my children, my friends, my work colleagues and so on – there is a ripple effect. This being the case, Sartre suggests that I need to consider this question: 'what would happen if *everyone* acted in this manner?'

At this point, Sartre seems to want to advocate a type of Kantian ethic. He seems to say that we should act as though our action was one that was a *reasonable* one for anyone else to carry out. Close reading, though, seems to suggest that Sartre offers a slightly different argument.

He suggests that when I undertake an action, I *must* believe that it is a reasonable action. If I do not, I am deceiving myself: in Sartre's terms, I am acting in 'bad faith'. The 'authentic' person, on the other hand, acknowledges that to choose a course of action *is* to imply that it is a 'right' action and, therefore, one that other people could reasonably be expected to carry out, too. If, for example, I *do* leave my wife and family and live on an island, I am saying something like 'in leaving my family and children and going to live on the island, I am doing a reasonable thing. It follows, then, that I cannot condemn anyone else who does the same thing.' There is a subtle difference, here, between the Kantian ethic and the Sartrean one. Kant seeks to establish that there are 'universal principles' that determine ethical decisions. Sartre, on the other hand, suggests that *individuals* are constantly determining the nature of 'right' actions. In being faced, constantly, by decisions and choices, people are determining on a dynamic basis what is right and wrong. This is a very 'fluid' view of ethics and suggests that ethics are situational. I cannot lay down, *a priori* a set of rules or principles for action because I am still in the process of 'inventing myself'. All I can do is to note that every time I act, I am saying to other people, via my actions, that 'this is a reasonable thing to do'.

All this leads us back to helping. To cut a very long story short, I continue to help because I continue to endorse help as 'right action'. I may not do so tomorrow and my beliefs and judgements may change as I evolve as a person but, for today, I believe that helping is important. Further, I hope that other people's actions – in as far as they affect me – will also involve helping. I would hope that others would help me although I cannot guarantee that they will. Although I cannot even *expect* that they will help, I will continue to hope. In this way, I am also supporting the idea of helping as a positive activity. It is something I would wish *on* other people and *for* other people – at least for the moment.

One of the most liberating – if daunting – features of existentialism is its *dynamic* quality. People, as defined by existentialists, are always in a state of flux: they are always engaged in the process of *becoming*. The human project is never complete. In this sense, we can never define, once and for all, what we *should* or *must* do. All we can do is to continue to review and reaffirm our beliefs – almost on a day-to-day basis. Helping, in this sense, becomes something of an act of faith.

Spiritual issues

As we have noted, a third approach to the question of why we should help lies in the spiritual domain. The whole issue of what 'spirituality' might be referring to is a complex one. While the word, itself, contains another word *spirit*, the term has been used more broadly than one to connote simply a belief in the inherent *spirit* of a person. It is, however, most frequently linked to religion and to religious beliefs.

What is important, here, is that religions, necessarily, hold that their beliefs about the nature of things – even supernatural things – are *true*. This poses something of a paradox. For, on the one hand, religious beliefs are necessarily just that – beliefs. On the other hand, the religious person holds those beliefs to be *true*. Thus, for the religious person, *beliefs* have become *truths* – and truths, by definition, are not beliefs but *facts*. It is hardly surprising, therefore, to note the amount of conflict that has occurred between people of different religions, for – presumably – various but different *truths* cannot coexist alongside each other and still remain 'true'. What happens is that each person, if he or she is of an extreme temperament or cultural persuasion, holds *only* his or her set of beliefs to be true and, therefore, all others to be false. Herein lies the source of conflict.

However, there are numerous elements in different religions that are common. This is not to say that all religions amount to the same thing nor to suggest (as it is popular to suggest) that all religions have an 'element of truth in them'. Such a notion is as difficult to 'prove' as the tenets of the various religions, themselves. It is to note that there are features in most religions that are echoed in most others. One of those issues is the injunction that members of the faith should *help* one another. In all of the major world religions this idea of helping each other is paramount. Indeed, it would be difficult to imagine a religion – existent or created – that suggested otherwise. To *help*, therefore, lies as an essential 'regulation' of religious faiths. It follows, therefore, that the 'religious' person is also one who helps. Not, interestingly enough, necessarily because he or she is a *person* but rather because he or she is a member of that religion or faith.

There is yet another way of looking at this question of helping from a religious perspective. It surrounds the issue of what we might understand when we use the word God. In the 1960s within Christianity, there was a considerable debate about the idea of religion without a formal sense of 'God up there or God out there (Robinson 1961) – the 'Honest to God' debate. Earlier – and firing this debate – Paul Tillich had described the idea of God in terms of the 'ground of our being' and his definition of God is worth considering at some length because it links so well with this discussion about religion and helping. Tillich wrote:

> The name of this infinite and inexhaustible depth and ground or all being is *God*. That depth is what the word *God* means. And if that word has not much meaning for you, translate it, and speak of the depths of your life, of the source of your being, or your ultimate concern, of what you take seriously without any reservation. Perhaps, in order to do so, you must forget everything traditional that you have learned about God, perhaps even that word itself. For if you know that God means depth, you know much about him. You cannot then call yourself an atheist or unbeliever. For you cannot think or say: Life has no depth! Life is shallow. Being itself is surface only. If you could say this in complete seriousness, you would be an atheist; but otherwise you are not. He who knows about depth knows about God.
>
> (Tillich 1949)

God, for Tillich, cannot be located 'above' the world, for 'above' can only exist when a 'flat earth' view of the universe is maintained. There can be no easy way of pointing 'up there' from our present view of the universe. To claim that there is an 'up there' would be rather like people in the UK trying to argue that people in Australia are upside down! But the depth of which Tillich writes is not a depth of some sort of universal geography but a *human* depth: a depth of experience, feeling and being.

If you are to accept Tillich's points about atheism and about knowing God, you must, of course, accept the first points that he makes – about God being 'the same as' depth. He rather seems to assume that the reader *will* make this 'leap of faith'. However, if the reader *does* accept Tillich's view of God, then the idea of *helping* takes on an even more urgent perspective. For the believer who sees God as the 'ground of our being' or in terms of depth is *required* to help another person simply because that other person *also* contains depth and also has God as the 'ground' or his or her being. It would seem that within Tillich's conception of God is contained the imperative to help each other. For not to do so is to care less about God.

At a more straightforward level, however, it is possible to note that most religions have a 'code of conduct' – usually written into holy books – that *prescribes* help for others. To help, in this case, is to follow the teachings of that particular religion by reference to its code of conduct. In this sense, the religious view of helping is very much akin to the *moral* view of helping.

But what of the atheist? While Tillich wants to dismiss atheism or a positive disbelief in the existence of God, others *would* acknowledge that such an unbelief is possible. How might the atheist answer the question 'why should I help?'

He or she might, of course, simply reply 'I won't! I have no reason to!' and that might be the end of the matter. Undoubtedly, for a few people, this is a tenable position and one that is consistent with the notion that there is not an outside force or higher being or ground of our being. However, the fact of being atheist does not *automatically* rule out the necessity to help.

It is interesting to note the position adopted by the *rational human-ists* (Blackham 1961) on this matter. They, as atheists, argue the following position. First, God – as far as they can tell – does not exist. Second, because of this fact, we are alone and responsible for what we do. Third, because of *this* fact, we are bound, not only to be respon-sible for ourselves but also for the whole of mankind. The rational humanist position has something in common with the existentialist position and much in common with the Kantian imperative. The fact that there is no 'outside arbiter' of what is right or wrong and no-one from whom forgiveness can be sought means that we must forge our own morality. We *must* help each other for *not* to do so is not to acknowledge and respond to the humanity in others. Thus, it may be argued, the atheist position does not exclude the idea of helping for self and others.

There are two other positions that might be considered in this brief review of religious and non-religious positions. They are *agnosticism* and what I want to call *spiritual neutrality*. The agnostic is the person who believes that, because the existence or otherwise of God can never be proved or disproved, discussion on the matter is irrelevant. We are only ever dealing with matters of *faith* and the question of God can never, ultimately, be verified. The agnostic, then, is the person who has dismissed religion, consciously, as being beyond debate and argument. More commonly, however, the term is used in an everyday sense to indicate the person who is 'not sure': the person who has yet to make up his or her mind about religious matters.

The question of *spiritual neutrality* is a different one. I want to suggest that for a considerable number of people – particularly in the West – the issue of spirituality and religion has little or no relevance. They simply do not weigh up the world and/or humanity in religious or spiritual terms. Religion and spirituality have little or no meaning for them. It is easy, in these days of discussions about 'spiritual needs' to assume that (a) *all* people have spiritual needs of one sort or another – even if these have yet to be identified and (b) that spiritual matters of one sort or another are, ultimately, important to *everyone*. A common argument, amongst those who *do* think about religion and about spiritual issues is to claim that such people have yet to give thought to these issues but that, at some unspecified time, they *will*. This becomes an impossible argument for it is never possible to specify *when* that sort of moment might occur! It seems to me, from the experience of looking after and helping a range of different sorts of people that, for some, spiritual matters – *however those matters are defined* – are irrelevant.

Again, neither of these positions necessarily or logically leads to one of lack of help. It seems quite possible to be an agnostic and to help or to be someone who is spiritually neutral and to help. Indeed (without retreating from the positions so far outlined) it is quite possible to argue that many people will help simply because they choose to do so. Why? Possibly because helping, itself, is *enjoyable*. In all the rather heavy debate about motives, attitudes, spiritual and non-spiritual issues, it is sometimes possible to lose sight of the sheer pleasure that helping others can offer. Nor need this be a *selfish* pleasure.

I remember, as a child, being impressed by how often my parents would go without things in order to pay for things for me. At the time, I imagined that they were incredibly altruistic (although, at the time, I would not have used that word!). I also thought that they must be martyrs to go without things for themselves in order to give things to me and my sisters. Now I am a parent of teenage children, however, I appreciate that no heroism or martyrdom is involved. It is simply pleasurable to give to your children. You do not give anything up, you do not think in terms of 'going without', you simply enjoy the giving. I propose that this can also be the motivation behind many acts of helping as a person. There *may* be deep-seated religious, cultural or even psychological motives but there may, simply, be the simple, human act of helping that creates pleasure in both the helper and the one who is being helped.

The answer to the question 'why help?' may come in various forms. We have explored the idea that helping may be a contractual issue. You help because that is what is expected of you and that is what your job consists of. Put less crudely, you help because the essence of being human is the helping relationship. Not to help is not to be fully involved in being human.

The question has also been tackled from an ethical point of view. It has been suggested that it is possible to argue from a variety of ethical positions that helping is some sort of moral imperative. We help others because we *must*. Or to put it another way, we are able to reflect on our own humanity and we are able to recognise the humanity of others. Once we realise that the world is peopled with creatures very like ourselves, we feel (or should feel) the need to treat those 'others' as we would want to be treated ourselves. This issue could, of course, have been opened up in other directions. There have been various *psychological* arguments for the need to treat other people helpingly. Freud, for example, posited the idea of a *superego* that 'controlled' our moral actions. Further, he suggested that we 'inherited' our morality from our parents and from the society in which we grew up and that our 'superegos' were largely manifestations of our consciences. We act helpingly because not to do so is to invoke a guilty conscience. Living with a guilty conscience may be more difficult than trying to live morally and than trying to help other people.

The question of 'why help?' has also been explored from a spiritual or religious perspective. These two concepts seem inextricably bound up with one another. I have argued, elsewhere, that the concept of 'spirituality' can be broadened to include the needs of atheists and agnostics and that it may not, necessarily, be linked with religion and with religious experience (Burnard 1987). I now feel that this is to extend the use of the term so widely as to make it almost meaningless. If the term 'spiritual' contains the word 'spirit' and if the word 'spirit' is linked very closely to religion (of whatever sort) then it seems to me, now, that spirituality and religion cannot be unlinked without stretching the terms almost irreconcilably. In this chapter, I have explored some of the ways in which helping becomes an imperative for the person who has religious beliefs. Often, this imperative comes from a given religion's code of conduct. At other times, though, it comes from beliefs about the nature of God. It also comes from most religions' teachings.

Finally, I have considered the position of helping from the point of view of agnostics and from the view of those for whom spiritual and religious issues have little meaning. I have suggested that helping can be pleasurable and worthy of pursuit for its own sake. In outlining this position, I would want to add that I am not suggesting the idea of the 'pleasurableness' of helping in terms of some sort of 'return' but that helping can give unselfish and even 'unrewarding' pleasure.

However it is viewed, it would seem that helping is an almost universal phenomenon and one linked to the very process of becoming and being a person. If that is the case, then helping remains at the centre of the process of being human for, whatever it is *not*, being human is intimately bound up with all aspects of the person.

Counselling and personal values

When we counsel or help another person, regardless of how open-minded we consider ourselves to be, we always run the risk of imposing our values on the other person. Like it or not and consciously or not we all live our lives according to some stated or unstated code or set of values. The idea that we can listen to another person and avoid judging what they say – even to a minimal degree – seems, to me, to be impossible. Because we hold a particular set of values, we are likely to think of those values as 'right'. If this were not the case, presumably, we would change them! However, our set of values may not be that of the person we counsel or help. Indeed, the client's values may be quite different to our own. Alternatively, the client's value system may be similar to ours and this can be equally difficult. When the counsellor's or helper's value system is similar to the client's we can be lulled into a sort of cosy collusion with the other person: the client merely uses the counsellor to confirm that his or her world view is the correct one and the counsellor is happy to oblige. Further, the counsellor is reinforced in his or her world view, for here is a person who holds the same values as himself or herself.

How do we cope with this 'values question'? First, I believe, by acknowledging that it is there and by refusing to delude ourselves that we operate in some sort of value-free arena when we try to help others. Second, by – as far as possible – suspending our own set of values during the counselling or helping session: no easy task. Third, by being as clear as we can about what our values are. I suspect that we can be clear about the most obvious ones but less clear about the ones we feel deeply or we feel shaky about. Sometimes, too, we hold oddly conflicting values. While we may feel that we live consistent lives and hold ourselves to a reasonably constant set of beliefs about how we should act, there are often times when we act contrary to that set of beliefs. In other words, we make mistakes, act inconsistently or just plain misbehave. All of these things, to my mind, are what make us human and it should, perhaps, please us that we are less consistent than we may want to be. Rather than struggling with this inconsistency, we may, instead, learn to live with it. The hard part, though, is *noticing* when we are inconsistent. Again, we can do this when our behaviours and values clash on the larger issues (for instance if we steal something but also believe that stealing is wrong) but it is harder to spot when less consciously held values are challenged by our behaviour. Often, all that we are left with when this happens is a sense of unease or anxiety that 'something has happened' or that we have 'not acted quite as we should'. The idea of the 'wounded healer' comes to mind here. We should not assume that by acting in the capacity of counsellor or helper we are somehow morally or even personally 'better' than the people we help. In the end, we are just as prone to making mistakes, falling foul of what we believe in and worrying about the consequences. It is probably the case that people who do make plenty of life mistakes end up being more effective counsellors and helpers.

This chapter closes with a Values Questionnaire, developed by the author, which may help you to think about your own value system.

Values Clarification Questionnaire

Clarifying our values can help us to deal with the variety of ethical dilemmas that face us in our personal lives and our professional lives as counsellors and helpers. Uncertainty over values can add to stress in counsellors and helpers by making decision making difficult.

This questionnaire may be used by a person working on their own who wishes to try to identify what they do and do not hold to be important. Alternatively, it can be used in a group or workshop setting as the basis for discussion and values clarification.

Work fairly quickly through the items in the questionnaire thinking about whether you strongly agree, agree, feel uncertain, disagree or strongly disagree with each one.

1   Clients should be allowed to read their case notes.
2   Abortion is always wrong.
3   Religious beliefs should always be respected no matter what the circumstances.
4   Gay people should be allowed to 'marry'.
5   People should be allowed to refuse psychiatric treatment.
6   Individuals always know what is best for themselves.
7   Wherever possible, children should have two parents.
8   Smokers should be held responsible for their own smoking-related diseases.

9   I should be able to choose not to work with people with AIDS.

10 Terminally ill people should have the right to end their own lives.

11 People are basically good.

12 Suicide is always wrong.

13 The age of consent should be lowered.

14 A nationalised health-care system is better than a private one.

15 All censorship is wrong.

16 People should be free to express their sexuality according to their preference.

17 Certain religious organisations should be outlawed.

18 The legal system is generally too lenient.

19 Psychiatric illness is caused as much by social factors as any others.

20 Clients should be prepared to pay something towards their treatment.

21 All children should be offered sex education in schools.

22 Racial prejudice exists in everyone.

23 Political organisations of every complexion should be allowed a say on television.

24 Alcoholics are not 'ill'.

25 I agree with most of the policies of the present government.

26 Parents should be responsible for the actions of their children.

27 Relatives should always care for sick relatives.

28 Some religious faiths are 'wrong'.

29 Capital punishment should be available for certain crimes.

30 Contraceptives should be available on demand.

3 Listening as the basis of counselling and helping

A question that often arises in the literature about counselling and helping is 'what are the *personal qualities* that make a good counsellor?' If such qualities could be isolated, then, presumably, it would be easier either to select people to be counsellors and helpers who had these qualities or it may be possible to train people to develop supposed latent qualities. The idea of isolating personal qualities, in this way, may in one sense be seen as excluding certain people from the tasks of counselling or helping. After all, if you do not have the required qualities, then it would be reasonable to assume that you should not be counselling or helping. I suspect, though, that our requirements of a helper vary to some degree. What *you* want from a helper in terms of personality, may not be what *I* want.

On the other hand, it seems reasonable to suggest that some people, by virtue of their personalities are likely to be better at helping than others. One would not, I imagine, want to argue that a sadistic, selfish and self-centred person was likely to make a good helper. In this chapter, I begin by exploring the issue of the personal qualities of a helper – by reference to a research study that I carried out. I go on to identify certain basic *skills* of counselling. Again, it is important that we are cautious when referring to such skills for, as we have identified in an earlier chapter, counselling and helping is not simply a question of rehearsing and exercising a range of mechanical skills. In the end, what seems to matter most of all is that there is a real 'person' behind the skills.

In a study in which we asked the question: 'what does an interpersonally skilled person "look like"', of a wide range of health-care workers it was found that it was not *skills* that were identified but the personal qualities of others that were described as important 'ingredients' of an interpersonally skilled person (Morrison and Burnard 1997).

A basic cluster of qualities of the effective counsellor was described by Rogers as: warmth, genuineness and transparency, acceptance and empathy (Rogers 1967). Later in the same volume, Rogers discussed the quality of unconditional positive regard for the client by the counsellor. It could be argued that Rogers extrapolated too far from his research findings in claiming that certain personal qualities were *necessary and sufficient* qualities for therapeutic change. This is a very strong claim indeed, for Rogers was claiming that by simply having these personal qualities a counsellor can be therapeutically effective. This point rarely seems to be challenged in the literature but Newell (1994) is an exception to this when he writes that there is:

> little clear evidence to demonstrate that Rogers'...'necessary and sufficient conditions' for effective therapy (warmth, empathy and genuineness) are either necessary or sufficient.

Newell's claim seems to hold up: I could find no further evidence of Rogers' original claim of 'necessary and sufficient' status being empirically supported. Nor does it seem likely that it would be possible to isolate, so clearly, these personal qualities as being the most important ingredients in the counselling process.

With these studies in mind, it was planned to explore students' perceptions of the personal qualities attributable to counsellors by health-care students. The overall aim was to identify to what degree similarities and differences would be identified between students' own choices of qualities and those identified in the literature. It was reasoned, too, that if health-care students were to develop counselling skills as prescribed by the literature, it would be interesting to note what sort of qualities those students deemed important in a counsellor. It was also felt to be interesting to identify in what ways perceptions of personal qualities might have changed since the studies of Rogers and Truax and Carkuff carried out in the 1960s. It was not intended that findings from the study would be generalisable, nor that they would support the notion of certain qualities offering necessary and sufficient conditions for therapeutic change.

Aim of the study

The aim of the study was to explore health-care students' perceptions of the personal qualities expected of a counsellor. It may be claimed that students are less influenced by the organisational culture of the hospital or community setting and are likely to have less experience of counselling than trained, management or educational staff and thus have a relatively fresh view of the topic.

The term 'counsellor', as we have noted, is open to various interpretations so, in this case, it was defined, stipulatively, as 'the sort that a person might go to see to talk about personal or emotional problems'. This was to differentiate between a counsellor as helper and confidante and other sorts of counsellors such as coaches, information-givers, trainers and supervisors. This is not to say that certain personal qualities do not apply to these categories of people but to acknowledge that most of the research that has been carried out into the personal qualities of an effective counsellor has been done on counsellors of the sort described above.

Sample

A sample of 200 students, on a range of health-care courses, were surveyed. Respondents were not required to identify themselves by course or by name, thus ensuring confidentiality. The sample was also self-selecting in as much as students could choose whether or not they completed the form. There were 162 usable survey papers returned – a response rate of 81 per cent.

Respondents were asked to identify up to ten personal qualities that they might expect to find in a counsellor. They were given the following instructions:

> I am interested in your views about what you feel are the *personal qualities* that could reasonably be expected to be found in a counsellor. A 'counsellor' in this case is the sort that a person might go to see to talk about personal or emotional problems.
>
> I would be grateful if you would list, below, the personal qualities that *you* would expect to find in a counsellor. There are no right or wrong suggestions but please bear in mind that this study focuses on *qualities* and not on *skills* or *qualifications*. You can list as few qualities as you like but please list no more than ten.

Despite the request to list 'no more than ten' qualities, a number of students identified more than ten. These other qualities were included in the analysis. The range of qualities identified by individual respondents was three to fifteen.

All of the responses were listed in a word-processing file. These items were then placed in alphabetical order to facilitate frequency counting of the various items. From this list it was possible to manually count the number of occurrences, within the total sample, of various personal qualities identified by the students. Percentages were then calculated and the findings placed in rank order.

A minimal amount of 'tidying up' of the data was carried out by putting all phrases in the same tense. Thus 'warmth' became 'warm' and 'respects other people' became 'respectful'. All variants of 'listens', 'listening', 'able to listen' became 'good listener'.

Among the most frequently identified qualities were those broadly in line with previous research and the literature: being non-judgemental, being empathic and understanding. However, other qualities, such as being approachable, sympathetic and caring rated highly, too. Often, empathy is identified in the literature as an important personal quality where sympathy is not. However, these items represent abstractions and, as such, may be difficult to define clearly. The novelist, Will Self identifies this problem, as follows:

> What do you think that the definition of 'empathy' is? Jot it down on a scrap of paper if it helps you to fix it in your mind. Now go and look these two definitions up in the dictionary. I think you'll find that you've got them the wrong way round, that what you thought was empathy is really is really sympathy and vice versa. You see, that's been my problem – all the time I thought I was sympathizing I was really empathizing. I'm not going to make big claims about this semantic quirk but I do think it's worth remarking on, for when two key terms bumble over one another in this fashion you can be sure that something is afoot.
>
> (Self 1994)

Safety and ethical qualities also appeared to be important (such as being confidential, trustworthy and honest). It should be noted, too, that some respondents addressed the issue in terms of 'negatives' (e.g. counsellors should be non-threatening, non-patronising or not forceful). The surprise 'quality', perhaps, was *good listener*: 73 per cent of the sample identified 'good listener' as a personal quality. As we shall see, in the discussion below, this runs counter to much of the literature which defines listening as a skill rather than as a quality. Table 3.1 identifies the range of findings down to qualities identified by at least five respondents.

Table 3.1 Qualities of counsellors as identified by students (number = 162)

Quality	Number	Per cent
Good listener	119	73
Non-judgemental	93	57
Empathic	56	35
Understanding	56	35
Approachable	43	27
Sympathetic	32	20
Caring	31	19
Friendly	31	19
Patient	28	17
Confidential	27	17
Supportive	22	14
Knowledgeable	19	12
Honest	18	11
Trustworthy	16	10
Experienced	12	7
Kind	12	7
Warm	12	7
Calm	11	7
Helpful	9	6
Respectful	8	5
Sense of humour	8	5
Advice giving	7	4
Considerate	7	4
Genuine	7	4
Open	7	4
Open-minded	7	4
Professional	7	4
Non-patronising	6	4
Objective	6	4
Reassuring	6	4
Trusting	6	4
Broad-minded	5	3
Comforting	5	3
Communicative	5	3
Relaxed	5	3

Discussion: is listening a quality or a skill?

The findings reported here highlight an interesting ambiguity. Although
the literature on counselling often identifies listening as a skill (see,

for example, BAC 1989a. 1989b; Davis and Fallowfield 1991; Morrison and Burnard 1997), many of the respondents, in this study, identified it as a *personal quality*. This is all the more clearly underlined by the fact that, at the top of the response sheet was the indication that the researcher was interested only in *personal qualities* and not in *skills*, as discussed above.

It is made more interesting by the fact that no other skills were identified in this way. If the respondents were generally mistaking or confusing qualities for skills, it would be likely that they would identify *other* skills in this way.

Thus it would appear, for these respondents at least, the issue of skills versus qualities merges when it comes to listening. This ambiguity is hinted at, but not made explicit, in a British Association for Counselling Code of Conduct which makes an apparent demarcation between 'listening skills' and 'counselling skills':

> The term 'counselling skills' does not have a single definition which is universally accepted. For the purpose of this code, 'counselling skills' are distinguished from 'listening skills' and from 'counselling'. Although the distinction is not always a clear one, because the term 'counselling skills' contains elements of these two activities, it has its own place between them...
>
> (BAC 1989a)

Although the BAC is not particularly clear on the issue – partly, as it admits, because the issue, as they find it, *is* not clear – they hint at a distinction between listening skills and counselling skills as two, possibly discrete, categories. The present findings seem to lend weight to an argument for not making such a clear distinction between 'listening', 'counselling skills' and 'personal qualities'. Listening, it would seem, may straddle a distinction between skills and personal qualities and leaves, in the air, the question: 'is listening a skill or a quality'? For the moment, though, we should note that the BAC, in the quotation, above, is still considering listening as a *skill*.

The question of whether or not listening is a skill or a personal quality is not easily answered and it may be noted that at least one writer offers a definition of listening that seems to indicate something more complex – and perhaps more personal – than mere skill:

> Listening is the complex, learned human process of sensing, interpreting, evaluating, storing and responding to oral messages.
>
> (Steil 1991)

It is notable, too, that in the study described here, an educator who also completed one of the survey forms commented, on the form, as follows:

> Qualities are very difficult to differentiate from skills because the personal qualities of a counsellor are often conveyed through competence in skills such as listening, empathic responding etc. etc.

It would seem possible, then, that personal qualities may be mediated through the demonstration of certain skills. On the other hand, it seems quite possible to rote learn a range of skills and *not* have the personal qualities behind those skills. The demonstration of skills does not offer conclusive evidence of particular qualities. The task of discerning underlying qualities or intentions from behaviour remains problematic.

If there is some slippage between the idea of a skill and the idea of a quality, we may want to consider, carefully, the implications of this for counselling training. This is discussed, further, below.

Conclusion

This section has offered an account of a descriptive study of students' perceptions of the anticipated personal qualities of counsellors. While the qualities that were identified by the respondents are broadly similar to those discussed in much of the counselling literature, the finding of an ambiguous response to whether or not listening was considered, by many respondents, to be a personal quality and/or a skill is an interesting one. By extension, it may be suggested that we might usefully consider whether the more familiar notion of a distinction between counselling skills and the personal qualities of counsellors may usefully be revisited.

The literature on counselling training often refers to the teaching of 'listening skills'. The suggestion is that, given practice and appropriate educational experiences, students can enhance their listening through rehearsing the skill. However, if listening is considered a quality or, perhaps, a quality and a skill, such an approach might have to be modified. For, it might be argued, personal qualities are not the sorts of characteristics that can so readily be honed by training.

It would seem possible that listening is more than simply a collection of behaviours to be learned. It is likely, too, that listening, in a therapeutic sense, involves more than just hearing and acknowledging the words spoken by another person. Arguably, though, many of the methods used to teach 'listening skills' are ones which focus on behavioural elements of the process: on sitting in a certain way, on maintaining eye contact, on using minimal prompts, on paying attention to non-verbal cues and so on.

While these are likely to be valuable in helping people to focus during the listening process, they do not, perhaps, capture some of the more subtle aspects of listening. We might argue, in the light of listening being considered a personal quality, that listening also involves a more subjective, difficult-to-pin-down aspect – perhaps akin to Martin Buber's notion of the meeting of two 'subjects' in the 'I–Thou' relationship (Buber 1958).

One possible solution to the issue of what constitutes a counselling skill and what constitutes a personal quality is to abandon the latter designation and to use the term *characteristic* in place of both. Thus we might talk of the 'characteristics of a counsellor' and that might include both skills and qualities. It is acknowledged, however, that this is, perhaps, a semantic 'fudge' and may only be a way of circumventing further debate on the importance, or otherwise, of the differences between human qualities and demonstrable skills. On the other hand, if we accept the point that 'personal qualities' may *not* play the major role in the counselling relationships and that skills are likely to be just as important, it may seem reasonable to merge the distinction between qualities and skills by the use of the term 'characteristics'.

This, in turn, may mean that some teachers of counselling skills to health-care professionals and volunteers may have to change their approach to such teaching. Given the emphasis, in the literature on 'counselling skills', the challenge may be to find ways of presenting the characteristics of an effective counsellor in such a way as to embrace both personal qualities and previously identified skills. Further, there might be discussion about whether or not it is *possible* to 'train' counsellors in particular personal qualities. While listening remains a skill, it seems possible to engage in skills training. If listening is more than a skill and merges, or becomes a quality, then we may or may not be able to engage in 'qualities training'. It seems likely that many people would claim that, by definition, personal qualities are more idiosyncratic and less visible than skills. Clearly, more work needs to be done to validate or reject the particular finding of this study.

What is listening?

All of this raises the question as to what counselling might be. If we forget, for a moment, the question of whether or not it can count as a skill or a quality, we might take a common-sense approach and note that, in one sense, it is simply hearing what another person is saying. However, this does not seem to take us very far. For even when we are simply hearing the words another person speaks, we are also *interpreting* what they are saying. Even with two people who are natural speakers of the same language, we cannot assume that each uses words in exactly the same way. The task for even the most casual listener is to try to work out what the other person *means* when he or she speaks. And herein lies a wealth of problems.

Some forms of psychotherapy involve a considerable amount of interpretation – far beyond understanding the words spoken. Those forms also involve 'reading between the lines' and trying to understand what a person is 'really' saying, beyond the words that they are using. Another point of view, however – and one that is being espoused here – is that it is more important, perhaps, to try to understand what the speaker is trying to convey. That is something different. It involves, if you like, a willingness to take what people say to you at face value. It means believing that this person in front of you is doing his or her best to convey to you what they mean. It also involves giving up a belief in any of our abilities to read a deeper meaning into what other people are saying. For it is my contention that it is impossible to understand the insides of other people's minds; that people vary in the ways in which they construe themselves and their worlds and that, therefore, it is more fruitful to allow the other person to *tell* you who and what they are. In this sense, then, listening involves trying, at some level, to look through the lens that the other person uses to view the world.

This is, of course, far easier to say than to do. We are probably all tempted to think that (a) our view of the world is largely the 'correct' one and that (b) other people think in similar ways to us. Perhaps one of the first lessons of counselling is to meet each person as a 'blank slate'; to make no assumptions about the other person until he or she enlightens us further about who they are. In this sense, every new counselling or helping relationship means starting from scratch, with no assumptions being made about the other person. To do this means to throw off stereotypes about people. It means the avoidance of judgement about what people look like, what they *might* be like and so on. It means meeting them as they are and discovering them as they reveal themselves to us. It is a truism, I think, that we know nothing about another person until that person begins to tell us who they are. This, then, is what is understood by listening in this context. It is hearing the other person's story, as it is described and conveyed by them, without judgement and without trying to 'dig beneath the surface'. The story that is being told – however clearly or obliquely – is the true story of this other person. We may, as we listen, note contradictions, paradoxes and confusions but this is all part of the other person's personal story.

Listening is probably the most important aspect of counselling and this may help to explain the finding, in the above study, of the students talking about listening as a quality rather than as a skill. Listening is far more than simply hearing a string of words: it is being able to assemble those words so that a picture emerges of another person's life. It is *not* the ability to interpret the other person's words in terms of a particular ideology or theoretical position. It is *not* the ability to understand the 'real' motives behind what another person is saying. It is the gradual gathering in of information about another person rather as a person constructs a jigsaw – only the puzzle is never completed. There are too many pieces that do not fit and just as we piece one set of bits together, something else is said to suggest that the pieces do not fit quite as neatly as we first thought. To listen is to accept ambiguity, to acknowledge that people are 'messy' and are not, necessarily, consistent. Real listening is probably, in the end, a mixture of both skill and personal ability.

Presumably we have learned, to varying degrees, the ability to listen. It would be difficult to argue that some people are born with the ability to listen better than others. It seems likely that we learn to listen from the examples we see around us. Those of us who have been listened to, perhaps, may be better at listening to others. Those of us who have never really felt understood by another person may find listening difficult. Also, I suspect, a certain patience is involved. For listening does involve patience. When we listen, we have to resist the temptation to jump in and finish sentences for the other person. We must also try to resist any urge to say, too quickly 'ah! I understand what you are *trying* to say'. What the person is trying to say is what they are saying: no more and no less. Patience is also involved in the fact that to listen is to give yourself and your time up to another person. For while we are listening to another person, we are not talking about ourselves. Intense listening involves a certain lack of ego and a disinclination to offer our own point of view.

Listening of any quality is far from being a passive activity. If we really listen and concentrate on another person, it can be hard work –

if only because of the 'bracketing' of our own thoughts and feelings that we have to engage in – the fact that we have to lay any preconceptions about this other person to one side for the period of listening.

The behavioural aspects of listening

There are various things we can do to show that we are listening (although, it is also true that listening is more than simply 'appearing' to listen). First, we may want to sit opposite the person we are listening to. This enables us, first and foremost, to maintain comfortable eye contact with them – a sure sign, perhaps, that we are listening. It also allows us to take account of their body language and to note, for example, when they are relaxing and when they are becoming anxious. We probably respond to these body language cues at an almost intuitive level.

The question of eye-contact in listening is an important one. Because, as counsellors or helpers, we are in a dominant position *vis-à-vis* the client – simply because of our differing roles – it is likely that we will make more eye contact than the client feels comfortable with. It is a useful rule of thumb to try to match the amount of eye contact that the client offers us. As the client comes to trust us more and to relax in our company, it is likely that he or she will increase the amount of eye contact made.

It has been suggested that an open sitting position, with arms and legs uncrossed, also helps to convey that the counsellor is listening to the client. However, the degrees to which people do or do not cross their arms and legs varies enormously across patterns of individual behaviour and across cultures. There are, for example, cultures in which crossing your legs is viewed as rude, whatever the context. Also, it is not uncommon for people to fold their arms as a way of concentrating on what they are doing. Advice about the open position may best be viewed as a base-line for observing your own non-verbal behaviour. If you find that you are tensing up and then folding your arms and legs, this may be a message to you that you are becoming defensive and a sign that it is time for you to take a deep breath and to slowly 'unwind' your body posture.

As a guide to good listening behaviours, it is worth observing chat show hosts on television. Clearly, their main task is to get their guests to relax and to talk. To aid this happening, they are often extremely skilled in the way that they present themselves to their guests. Observe them and you may well learn how to enhance your own presentation of self to your clients.

Body language

Over the past few decades, much attention has been paid to the notion of body language. Body language, or non-verbal communication has come to refer to at least the following:

- gestures
- eye
- paralinguistic aspects of speech (anything in speech other than words)
- posture
- sitting position.

Borrowing from various sources, a number of writers have attempted to map out what body language might 'mean'. The difficult thing, here, is that non-verbal aspects of behaviour develop out of various contexts: socialisation, role-modelling, personal preference, habit and so on. It is, therefore, difficult to develop a general theory of what any particular set of body movements might mean. It is important to explore your own views on this issue but it may be useful, also, to remain sceptical of the degree of accuracy that can be brought to bear when attempting to 'interpret' non-verbal behaviour. My own feeling is that, in the end, our non-verbal behaviour is so personalised as to be difficult for another person – or even ourselves – to develop any particular theories about what it means. Also, I suspect that a fair amount of our non-verbal behaviour happens arbitrarily: we cross our arms, for instance, for no particular reason, we smile in the wrong places, we cross and uncross our legs because we feel more or less comfortable that way. To slip into these movements being linked, directly, with internal or psychological states represents a certain leap of faith.

There are also *cultural* differences in the use of non-verbal behaviours. In some cultures, for instance, it is not appropriate for the 'junior' person in conversation with another to make direct eye contact with the senior. In other cultures, it is the case that people look away as they are speaking and make eye contact when they are listening; in yet other cultures, these two roles are reversed. Much of the literature on non-verbal behaviour appears to be ethnocentric and often refers to what is perceived as common behaviour in Europe and North America. Margaret McLaren deals with this topic sensitively and usefully in her book *Interpreting Cultural Differences: the challenge of intercultural communication* (1998).

4 Models of the person

How we make sense of ourselves and other people is going to affect the ways in which we manage our lives and help others. There are various ways of making sense of experience and of being a person and this chapter explores some of them in relation to counselling and helping. It is not claimed that an exhaustive list of models of the person is offered but the aim is to stimulate debate and thought about what drives someone to help another person and about how people who are asking for help may or may not construe the world. Nor should these models necessarily be viewed as being mutually exclusive. Some are: it would be difficult to find common ground, for instance, between seeing the person as exercising free will and the person as being subject to fate. Some, on the other hand, can live side by side: it is quite possible to see the person as agent *and* to view them as attempting to achieve their potential.

The person as driven by their past

This is the classical psychodynamic model as perhaps best exemplified in the writings of Sigmund Freud and his followers. The argument, in the model, goes something like this. The material or physical world is everywhere and always subject to causal law. It would be difficult, for example, for me to argue that the computer I am using to write these words just suddenly 'appeared' in the world. Most people would acknowledge that before it was a computer, it was a series of metal, plastic and other parts and before the metal in it was steel, it was ore. Thus it is possible, at least in theory, to trace all objects back to their roots. Everything is part of a causal chain. So, according to this model, are minds and people. Everything we are thinking about ourselves, today, is necessarily linked to how we felt yesterday and, in turn, how we felt as children. This is sometimes called *psychic determinism*.

The term 'psychic' here is not used in any mysterious sense: it is simply used to denote the mind. Thus our minds and our personalities are necessarily dependent on past events, thoughts and feelings. It follows, then, that the way to sort out problems in the present, is to trace them to their roots in the past.

In a way, this way of thinking about people has entered popular culture. It is often claimed, for example, that those people who are abused as children are likely to grow up as abusers themselves. Similarly, many people feel that you can find the answer as to why the adult is as he or she is by looking back at the childhood.

The counsellor working with such a framework is likely to place great emphasis on helping the client to explore his or her past and will, perhaps, work at 'resolving' past difficulties by helping the client to face them or even to 'relive' them.

The person as agent

This model of the person is almost diametrically opposed to the previous one. The argument, here, is that people exercise *free will*. That means that people are capable of choosing what they do or think. They can do this, perhaps, because they have *consciousness*. Rather than simply being led by their past, the fact that they can think about themselves and their predicaments means that they can 'over-ride' any 'programming' of the past.

Philosophically, this approach can be traced back, at least, to the existential philosophy of the French philosopher, Jean-Paul Sartre, who argued that we are both free and responsible for what we do. He claimed, too, that no one can choose our lives for us: we are *agents* and, in a way, we write our own lives as we go along. We are the authors of our personalities: there is no blueprint for how we will be in the future and there is no absolute reason why we should allow the past to influence the way we are in the present – except if we *choose* to do so.

It is this sort of thinking that lies behind the client-centred approach to counselling, as exemplified by Carl Rogers. Indeed, his biography suggests that Rogers was something of a convert to existentialism from Christianity at quite an early age. The client-centred approach to counselling stresses the need for the counsellor to refrain from 'leading' the client and the need for the counsellor to help the client to both identify his or her own problems and to choose the solutions to them. Of course, as part of this process, the client may choose to explore his or her past and this is accounted for within the model. What is being claimed, here, is that it is the individual person who is responsible for how he or she explores his or her life and how, in future, he or she lives it. Within the client-centred model, there is no room for advice-giving by the counsellor and the approach emphasises the *differences* between people rather than the similarities.

One immediate problem with such an approach is that if we say that everyone is an individual, then it becomes very difficult to develop 'theories about the person': each person, after all, has their own theoretical make up. Perhaps what Rogers argued best was that counsellors should 'stay out of the way' of clients and enable them to choose their lives for themselves.

The person as scientist

The personal construct psychologist, George Kelly used the metaphor of the 'person as scientist' to elucidate a model of the person. Within this model, we are constantly making predictions about how the world and our lives are going to be (or identifying 'hypotheses') and then testing out our predictions according to how the world actually does turn out to be. In the light of our findings, we modify our hypotheses about the world. And so we continue through life via a series of predictions and tests. For example, I may hypothesise, at some time in my life (and perhaps based on past experience) that people cannot be trusted. I then test this out and find that *some* people can be trusted and are pleasanter than I thought. This, in turn, leads me to cast a new hypothesis along the lines of 'there are some people who can be trusted, while there are others who cannot'). Continuing the process, I act according to this new hypothesis until another life experience forces me either to confirm it or to change it.

The counsellor who works within this model may help the client to explore the way in which he or she views the world and how he or she hypothesises or construes what happens to him or her. In doing so, the counsellor may challenge the client for evidence of a particular point of view and thus, gently, help the client to validate or otherwise the hypotheses that he or she has developed. It seems quite possible that most of us carry around with us hypotheses that have not been fully tested or which could, if we thought about them, be modified in various ways.

The person as someone with potential to grow

Again, a popular theme in the Rogerian approach to counselling and popular, too, in New Age thinking, is the model of the person as having potential to grow. This model holds that few, if any of us, normally achieve our full potential and that we can, by various means, be helped further in this goal. Exactly how it is possible to predict that people have this potential is not made completely clear in the literature and, in some ways, this model rests on an act of faith: often that act is one that involves seeing the human project as a positive and life-enhancing one. According to this way of thinking, people, if given the time and opportunity, will always work towards what is 'right' for them. We are, if encouraged, born with a tendency towards the positive. Sometimes, this potential for positive growth is stunted – perhaps by unpleasant or disturbing life events. It is one of the counsellor's tasks to help the client to reclaim his or her ability to work towards positive ends.

This approach is in direct opposition to Freudian thinking of people as 'essentially aggressive' and of that behind certain world religions in which people are viewed as 'essentially bad' – although usually redeemable. The 'growth' model sees people as 'essentially good' and with the stated potential for further personal development and growth. The approach arose out of American, humanistic psychology and is most clearly described in the works of Carl Rogers and Abraham Maslow.

The person as essentially bad

This point of view is seen in a number of world religions. It covers the ideas of being 'born into sin' and being 'redeemable' by a belief in a god or higher power. The escape from sin, as it were, is dependent on the person's faith in this higher power. The psychologist, Erich Fromm, has suggested that religion thus offers something of a bargain: that it can relieve people from their sin and guarantee them a better after life.

The person as essentially good

This is the obverse of the previous belief system. Dating back, at least, to the philosopher Rousseau, it was developed, in this century, by the humanistic psychologist, Carl Rogers, who established the view that people tended to 'grow towards goodness' and to make 'right' rather than wrong decisions for themselves. A more detailed account of this position is offered above. It is interesting to note that Rogers adopted this position after abandoning theological studies.

The person as a social construction

This is a sociological and political point of view: that people are culturally and societally determined. In its strongest expression, the 'individual' is not important: what is important is the society which surrounds and shapes the person. It is arguable that those who see people as being socially constructed would have little time for counselling as a means of helping: the point, instead, would be to work on the political and societal conditions in which people live. Even if one did not accept this position, it offers an important point about the limitations of counselling: that it cannot change many of the social situations into which people are born or live.

Fatalism

Fatalism is the belief that God or some other power has mapped out our lives for us and that we are living according to some pre-planned schedule. Thus, what happens to me in the future is somehow and somewhere determined: I am on a particular life route and there is little that I can do to change it. This belief occurs in a number of world religions but should not be confused with determinism, as described above. Determinism refers to events leading to the present. Everything that I am, today, is related to what has gone before. But this does not necessarily mean that what will happen next is predetermined: simply that whatever happens will be linked to the present. The fatalistic point of view, however, holds that there is a blueprint for the whole of our lives and that, to a considerable degree, we are passive livers-out of that blueprint.

It is difficult to see how mainstream counselling, as viewed from the European or North American point of view can be compatible with fatalism. However, it can be noted that in many countries in which fatalism is part of the most common world view, there are often religious advisers who act as counsellors and who advise their clients on the basis of the writings contained in particular holy books. In this sense, then, the counselling offered is very directive and prescriptive. It amounts to advice about how the person might live more closely in line with the prevailing set of religious beliefs.

The person as being the sum of their behaviour

The most visible part of the person is his or her behaviour. Some would argue that *all* we are is our behaviour and that all aspects of our personality are learned. Thus, we learn how to love other people; we learn how to trust or distrust them; we learn how to get upset or be happy and so on. In this model of the person, there is no 'real self', hidden, as it were, beneath the outer shell of behaviour: we *are* our behaviour.

The positive aspect of this view is that as everything we are has been learned, so it can be unlearned. We are not programmed by our past or driven by our destiny, we can be helped to be different by changing our behaviour. The depressed person, for example, can be helped not to be depressed by changing those behaviours associated with that mood state. Examples of the behaviours associated with depression are tears, lethargy, negative statements and so forth. The person who works in a behavioural way will be able to help the person with depression by encouraging more positive and life-asserting behaviours and by ignoring the negative.

This approach is sometimes criticised on the grounds that it does not get to the root causes of distress. Those who subscribe to the behavioural model might argue that there is no way of knowing what – if any – the root causes there are to any given human condition. All that we need concern ourselves with is the behaviour experienced by this individual, now. This, then, is an exactly opposite view of the person from the one espoused by those who take the psycho-dynamic view.

The person shaped by their thinking

Similar to the model outlined above, this view offers one of the person being affected in day-to-day life by the way that he or she thinks. What we feel about ourselves or a situation is governed by what we think of ourselves or situations. The person who constantly thinks 'I am not a very intelligent person and pretty worthless as a human being' is likely to experience feelings of unhappiness and insignificance. The task of the person helping another person through this approach is to help in a change of thinking. Thus, a counsellor working this way might challenge the thinking process of such a person. He or she may say 'What evidence do you have for thinking that you are not intelligent?' and 'give me some examples of how you know you are worthless?' In this way, the counsellor helps the client to unpack some or his or her thought processes and gradually to replace them with more positive ones.

According to this approach to thinking about the person, we tend to generalise about ourselves from very little evidence. When we fall out with a person we like, there is a danger that we will employ the 'globalism' of 'nobody likes me'. We have generalised from the fact that we do not get on with one person to 'I don't get on with anyone'. Again, the task of the counsellor working from this point of view would be to help the client to examine these sorts of globalisms and to challenge what evidence exists to believe in them.

The person as an emotional being

A quite different approach is that of seeing the person as being to varying degrees driven by their emotions. Within this model is the view that we often repress or suppress our feelings and that such repression or suppression leads to emotional problems. Within this view of the person, it is seen as healthy that a person can express their feelings and emotions. It is not uncommon, therefore, in counselling that is undertaken from this point of view, for the client to express strong feelings through crying or expressing anger. It is probably true to say that this view has entered popular culture. It is widely held that 'emotions should be expressed rather than bottled up'. However, concrete evidence for belief in this statement is limited. Behaviourists might argue that the expression of emotion in this way simply leads to the reinforcement of such behaviour. Thus, the person who cries a good deal is simply learning how to cry more.

Exploring your own view of the person

In reading through the above thumbnail sketches of how people may be viewed, it is possible that you may feel that 'this one most closely matches what I feel about people' or 'I think there is some truth in each of them'. The point, of course, is to become aware of the assumptions that we make about 'human nature' as it applies to counselling and helping. It is also worth remembering that the person who comes for counselling or helping will also have *their* view of what makes a person tick. Both counsellor and client, in conversation, will 'meet' those views and sometimes there will be a difference of opinion about the 'true nature' of persons. When this happens, it is always worth taking some time away from the presenting problems to examine the person's philosophy of life and people. This is not to say that the conversation should turn into a detailed philosophical debate but simply to suggest that it is useful for both counsellor and client to clarify his or her views of the person.

It seems likely, too, that any given person will change the way they view human beings over time. A person who is formally trained in a particular world view may change when confronted with a different approach to people. Humanistic psychologists have been known to become behaviourists and vice versa. Perhaps, too, ideas about the nature of people change with age and through encountering other social, political and religious views, or the lack of them.

5 Basic counselling and helping strategies

As we saw in the last chapter, there is a range of theoretical approaches to understanding the person. I can summarise only a few of them here, but they do represent some of the different ways in which people have theorised about the nature of human beings. Whereas the last chapter offered 'freehand' sketches of the ways in which some people view other people, in this chapter, we explore, in more detail, the formalising of these sketches.

Perhaps the most longstanding approach to understanding people is the Freudian, psychodynamic approach. Dating back, at least, to the turn of the century, the psychodynamic approach conceptualises people as driven by their pasts. What I am in the present is, necessarily, a result of events that have happened to me previously. So it follows, in this paradigm, that if you want to understand the person's present problems, look to his or her past. The term that captures this approach is that of 'psychic determinism'. In the world around us, most things are subject to causal law. To use a simple example, we may take the book that you are reading. If we consider the physical fact of the book, we can say, with certainty, that before the book was composed of paper, that paper was produced from wood pulp. Before that wood pulp came into existence, the wood content was a tree. Before the tree, a seed, and so on. Similarly, before the words appeared in the book, they were typed on a computer, before that, they existed in my head and so on. So, for the psychodynamic school of thinkers, it is with human beings. Anything that exists in people's minds is necessarily preceded by other thoughts. Before a personal event happens, there is necessarily another human precursor to it. Thus Freud was able to argue that mental events, like physical ones, are subject to determinism or, to put it another way, are part of a causal chain.

This approach to thinking about people has stayed popular. Although, arguably, Freudian ideas have fallen out of favour, there is still a considerable tendency in 'Western' thinking to attribute human problems in the present to those in the past. Thus, child abusers tend to be thought of as probably having being abused themselves. Those with neurotic problems are thought to have had difficulties in their childhoods.

A different view of people was offered by the first behavioural psychologist, John B. Watson. He argued, in direct opposition to Freud, that in order to make a formal study of the person, psychology should abandon introspection. For Watson, the important thing was to study that which was observable about people: their behaviour. With B.F. Skinner – perhaps behaviourism's most famous practitioner and theorist – he argued that all human behaviour is learned. Putting it simply, we learn by being encouraged or by having our behaviour reinforced. Thus, I learned to tie my shoe laces by someone – a teacher or a parent, perhaps – praising me when I moved in any positive direction towards tying my laces. So it is with more complex human behaviours. I learned, arguably, to fall in love by meeting someone who encouraged me in feeling emotionally attached to them. And, similarly, they learned to fall in love with me by being so encouraged by me. According to the behaviourists, all human behaviour is learned and so it follows that all human behaviour can be unlearned. Out of all this arose a very prominent school of psychotherapy and counselling known as cognitive behaviour therapy. The principle behind this therapy is that our thinking informs our emotions: what we think about ourselves and the world affects how we feel about those domains of our lives. The cognitive behaviour therapist thus helps a client to check faulty thinking and so improve his or her emotional status. A simple example may suffice here. Many people tend to use 'globalisms' to describe how they feel about themselves. Thus, I may say to others: 'no one likes me'. This is a globalism. The 'fact' that may emerge out of cognitive behaviour therapy is that it is *not* the case that 'nobody' likes me but that I have come to believe this based on a couple of bad experiences with people. I have extrapolated from 'I don't get on with a few people', to 'no one likes me'. One of the tasks of the cognitive behaviour therapist is to help people to readjust the way in which they think about themselves and the world in order to clarify how they feel about those aspects of their lives.

A third approach to thinking about human beings arose in the late 1940s as a reaction to Freudian determinism and what was perceived as the rather mechanistic approach of behaviourism. This was what came to be known as humanistic psychology. Those involved in humanistic psychology argued that what we should concentrate on was how the *individual* viewed and made sense of the world. There could be no overriding theory that covered all human beings. What mattered, instead, was that we tried to understand how each of us, as individuals, viewed the world. Out of all this was born the client-centred approach to counselling (and psychotherapy) first introduced and developed by Carl Rogers, a humanistic therapist and educator. It is arguable that Rogers' approach to counselling has been the most pervasive for the past thirty years.

Rogers argued that it mattered less what the 'expert' felt about any given person's problems and more what that person made of their situation. He suggested that, given time and space, most of us could identify both our own problems and the solutions to them. Indeed, he argued, further, that it was *only* the individual who could do this work. This was based on a definite individualistic approach to thinking about human beings. The argument goes something like this. Each person views the world differently. None of us lives exactly the same life as anyone else. So it follows that we, as individuals, are the experts on our own particular situations.

The problem, perhaps, with such extreme individualism is an interesting one. If all of us are total individuals – 'one offs', as it were – then it becomes impossible to develop general theories about human beings. All we can say is that the world is peopled by a huge range of individuals, each of whom differs from the others. And yet Rogers *did* develop theories of human beings and *did* prescribe an approach to counselling. All of this leaves his position most debatable.

These, then, are thumbnail sketches of arguably the three most prominent views of human nature from a psychological perspective. It is interesting to view them from the perspective of the late twentieth century. I think that it is safe to say that Freudian views of the person are generally in decline. It is also safe to say, after Rogers himself, that the humanistic approach, although broadly adopted in counselling practice, never gained a real foothold in academic psychology, and that behavioural psychology – for whatever reason – has been the most pervasive. Certainly, in the late 1990s, if a person studies psychology at university, it is likely that he or she will study more behavioural and experimental psychology than psychodynamic or humanistic psychology.

The question now arises as to whether or not it is possible to practise counselling and helping *without* a particular theoretical perspective. While, in the pure sense, none of us works in the world without some sort of theoretical view, I still think that the answer to such a question can be 'yes'. I believe that we can adopt a pragmatic view of the human position and help people according to both their and our view of their needs at any given time. The person who comes to me for help on a particular problem *may* be helped if I take a particular theoretical view of their problem but my guess is that most of us are looking for something more immediate and practical. We are looking for ways of resolving our problems and of making life more liveable in the process. This resolution may or may not come via a helper adopting a given theoretical position. Resolution may come out of the helper looking around for practical strategies, with the person in question, and working out an achievable means of seeking problem resolution. This is not to say that I am advocating a complete blindness to and ignorance of psychological thought on matters of the person but merely to note that most of us want to sort ourselves out as painlessly and as practically as possible.

Feelings

Issues in counselling are often closely related to feelings. We bottle them up, we forget them, we have difficulty in expressing them or we express them in great abundance. Whilst stress affects different people in different ways it seems to be the case that very often it is because we cannot cope with our emotions that we feel very stressed. In this chapter the emotions are explored and practical methods of coping with them are offered.

Emotions

John Heron (1989) distinguishes between at least four types of emotion that are commonly suppressed or bottled up: anger, fear, grief and embarrassment. He notes a relationship between these feelings and certain overt expressions of them. Thus, in the stressed person, anger may be expressed as loud sound, fear as trembling, grief through tears and embarrassment by laughter. He notes, also, a relationship between those feelings and certain basic human needs. Heron argues that we all have the need to understand and know what is happening to us. If that knowledge is not forthcoming, we may experience fear. We need, also, to make choices in our lives and if that choice is restricted in certain ways, we may feel anger. Third, we need to experience the expression of love and of being loved. If that love is denied us or taken way from us, we may experience grief. To Heron's basic human needs may be added the need for self-respect and dignity. If such dignity is denied us, we may feel self-conscious and embarrassed. Practical examples of how these relationships 'work' in everyday life and in the health professions may be illustrated as follows:

> It helps if I can talk to somebody close to me. Sometimes I find that I am very mixed up and then I 'turn off'....I don't seem to care any more...

> I remember reaching the point were I was very angry with my patients....I obviously couldn't tell them...it was irrational really...

> Sometimes I feel very mixed up....I become so stressed that I don't know whether to laugh or cry...

In the last example it may be noted how emotions that are suppressed are rarely only of one sort. Very often, bottled-up emotion is a mixture of anger, fear, embarrassment and grief. Often, too, the causes of such blocked emotion are unclear and lost in the history of the person. What is perhaps more important is that the expression of pent-up emotion is often helpful in that it seems to allow the person to be clearer in their thinking once they have expressed it. It is as though the blocked emotion 'gets in the way' and its release acts as a means of helping the person to clarify their thoughts and feelings. It is notable that the suppression of feelings can lead to certain problems in living that may be clearly identified. We will note, later in this chapter, the effects that pent-up emotion can have. Before that, however, it is important to explore how another way of dealing with unpleasant feelings and thoughts is to deny them in certain ways. Here, the concept of mental mechanisms is useful.

Mental mechanisms

None of us can accept too much reality. The truth is often painful. Therefore we learn to cushion ourselves against the truth by the use of what have been called 'mental mechanisms'. These are usually associated with Freud, although other writers have also developed his original formulation. Mental mechanisms help us to guard against excessive anxiety and stress by allowing us some breathing space from the truth about either the way the world is or about the way others think or feel about us. Used sparingly, mental mechanisms are healthy – they can save us considerable, unnecessary pain and anguish. On the other hand, over-use of them can mean that we are taking avoiding action rather too often. The other problem arises when we are *unable* to use them – when we see the truth only too clearly. This too is a recipe for pain and distress. Some would argue that inability to use mental mechanisms at all leads to severe psychological breakdown. What, then, are examples of mental mechanisms?

Projection

Projection refers to the process whereby we see qualities in others that are our own, but of which we are unaware. Consider, for example, the following description of one social worker by another:

> She's a very good social worker….it's just that she has such a high opinion of herself…she always wants to talk about herself and never wants to listen to other people.

Now this *may* be an accurate description of the other person. Alternatively, it may say more about the commentator than it ever does about the person being described.

Notice, in future conversations, any tendency you have to project in this way. Note, too, that it is possible to project feelings onto the environment around us. Take, for example, the person who enters a pub and says 'this place has an interesting atmosphere'. Arguably, places do not have 'atmospheres'. Instead, we bring the atmosphere with us and project our own thoughts, preferences and feelings onto different environments. Thus the person who is describing a pub in this way is possibly projecting their own wishes and desires onto it.

Projection also happens in groups. The group member who constantly talks of the group's 'hostility' may often be projecting their own hostility onto the group. Rather than facing that personal hostility, it is safer to discover it in the world around them (i.e. the group). To take this a stage further, some find their own hostility so hard to bear that they project it onto the world at large. Thus they tend to see the world in general as a hostile place. In this case, the person's whole life is directed by the notion of the world being hostile. A moment's thought will reveal that, in literal terms, the 'world' *cannot* be 'hostile'.

As with all mental mechanisms, it is important to note two possibilities:

1 that projection is being used, *or*
2 the person who is apparently projecting is, in fact, offering a literal description of another person or thing.

Thus, to take the group example, the person who sees the group as 'hostile' may either be projecting their own feelings *or* they are identifying what is actually happening in the group. It would be unwise to see all human action and description as examples of the use of mental mechanisms. The secret and the skill lies in being able to differentiate between mental mechanisms and 'the truth'. The safest way of proceeding is possibly to avoid interpreting other people's utterances as mental mechanisms and to concentrate, instead, on our own motives and behaviours. Thus it is helpful for me to be able to identify when I am projecting feelings onto others. It is less helpful (and arguably impossible with any accuracy) for me to observe others doing it. Noticing my own tendency to project can help me to gain self-awareness and can aid in lowering stress levels by slowly coming to *face* the world rather than escape from it.

Rationalisation

Rationalisation occurs when a rational excuse is offered for behaviour or situations that are otherwise painful to accept. Consider this example of a student nurse who opens the letter that tells him he has failed his final examinations:

> I don't care really…anyway, no one could pass an examination after the training *we* had. No one ever helped you to get through exams…

Again, as with projection, two things *could* be happening here. The student could be rationalising his true feelings of disappointment at receiving bad news. Alternatively, he could be expressing truths about his training and his reactions to failing the exam! Again, it may be more helpful to notice your own tendency to rationalise in this way than it is to observe the possible rationalisations of others.

A degree of rationalisation helps us to avoid considerable anxiety, especially in the short term. In the long run, however, it is probably better that we learn to accept things as they really are and to avoid offering 'excuses' for what we do or feel. Identifying a tendency to rationalise excessively can be part of the process of becoming self-aware and such self-awareness can, in the long term, help us to reduce stress.

Reaction-formation

Reaction-formation is a rather different sort of mental mechanism. It is the process by which we sometimes express *exactly the opposite* feeling to the one that we really hold. Consider, for example, the person who moans about another and who says that if he were to meet him, he would tell him exactly what he thinks of him. Consider, too, when the pair meet and the one who has been moaning greets the other with: 'Hello David: it's good to see you again! How are you keeping?' This is one example of reaction-formation. Arguably what is happening here is that it is safer for the person to stay amicable with the other rather than face a show-down with the person that he dislikes.

A deeper and perhaps more sinister example of reaction-formation occurs when a person has a deep-seated anxiety about one aspect of his personality and deals with this by berating anyone else that has this personality aspect. Consider, for example, the person who 'hates' homosexuals and takes every opportunity to express that hatred whilst all the time he is denying homosexual tendencies in himself.

Again, it is possible to see the value of identifying our own tendencies towards reaction-formation. If we can identify the 'opposites' that exist within us we can come to know ourselves better. We can begin to appreciate that many of our prejudices and dislikes are related to ourselves.

Intellectualisation

Intellectualisation is a defence against emotion. The person who intellectualises is the one who constantly seeks a rational answer to everything rather than allowing that some things are 'felt' rather than 'known'. The educational systems in the West have typically favoured rationality above the emotions and it is hardly surprising, therefore, that the tendency is for many people to want logical explanations for events, behaviours and thoughts. The person who intellectualises, however, *over-uses* the logical sense and uses it to avoid having to face emotion.

The effects of bottling up emotions

In the discussion so far, we have considered the nature of the emotions and the ways in which we sometimes delude ourselves in order to save ourself further stress and discomfort. What, then, are the long-term and short-term effects of bottling up emotions?

Physical discomfort and muscular pain

Wilhelm Reich, a psychoanalyst with a particular interest in the relationship between emotions and the musculature noted that blocked emotions could become trapped in the body's muscle clusters (Reich 1949). Thus he noted that anger was frequently 'trapped' in the muscles of the shoulders, grief in muscles surrounding the stomach and fear in the leg muscles. Often, these trapped emotions lead to chronic postural problems. Sometimes, the thorough release of the blocked emotion can lead to a freeing up of the muscles and an improved physical appearance. Reich believed in working directly on the muscle clusters in order to bring about emotional release and subsequent freedom from suppression.

Trapped emotion is sometimes 'visible' in the way that the client holds himself and the skilled person can learn to notice tension in the musculature and changes in breathing patterns that may suggest muscular tension. We have noted throughout this book how difficult it is to interpret another person's behaviour. What is important, here, is that such bodily manifestations be used only as a clue to what may be happening in the person. We cannot assume that someone who looks tense, is tense, until they have said that they are.

Counsellors or helpers will be very familiar with the link between body posture, the musculature and the emotional state of the person. Frequently, if patients and clients can be helped to relax, then their medical and psychological condition may improve more quickly. Those health professionals who deal most directly with the muscle clusters (remedial gymnasts and physiotherapists, for example) will tend to notice physical tension more readily but all carers can train themselves to observe these important indicators of the emotional status of the person in their care.

Difficulty in decision making

This is a frequent side effect of bottled-up emotion. It is as though the emotion makes the person uneasy and that uneasiness leads to lack of confidence. As a result, that person finds it difficult to rely on his own resources and may find decision making difficult. When we are under stress of any sort it is often the case that we feel the need to check decisions with other people. Once some of this stress is removed by talking through problems or by releasing pent-up emotions, the decision-making process often becomes easier.

Faulty self-image

When we bottle up feelings, those feelings often have an unpleasant habit of turning against us. Thus, instead of expressing anger towards others, we turn it against ourselves and feel depressed as a result. Or, if we have hung onto unexpressed grief, we turn that grief in on ourselves and experience ourselves as less than we are. Often, in counselling, as old resentments or dissatisfactions are expressed, so the person begins to feel better about themselves.

Setting unrealistic goals

Tension can lead to further tension. This tension can lead us to set ourselves unreachable targets. It is almost as thought we set ourselves up to fail! Sometimes, too, failing is a way of punishing ourselves or it is 'safer' than achieving. Release of tension, through the expression of emotion, can sometimes help a person to take a more realistic view of himself or herself and his or her goal setting.

The development of long-term faulty beliefs

Sometimes, emotion that has been bottled up for a long time can lead to a person's view of the world being coloured in a particular way. They learn that 'people can't be trusted' or 'people always let you down in the end'. It is as though old, painful feelings lead to distortions that become part of that person's world view. Such long-term distorted beliefs about the world do not change easily but may be modified as the person comes to release feelings and learns to handle emotions more effectively.

The 'last straw' syndrome

Sometimes, if emotion is bottled up for a considerable amount of time, a valve blows and the person hits out – either literally or verbally. We have all experienced the problem of storing up anger and taking it out on someone else: a process that is sometimes called 'displacement'. The original object of our anger is now replaced by something or someone else. Again, the talking through of difficulties or the release of pent-up emotion can often help to ensure that the person does not feel the need to explode in this way.

Positive ways of coping with emotions

So far, we have discussed only the negative ways of dealing with emotion. Heron (1989) identifies what he calls six 'positive' emotional states. These are: identification, acceptance, control, redirection, switching and transmutation. An understanding of the six can help in a broader understanding of how we may cope with emotional stress.

Identification

In this case, the person is aware of his or her emotional status. Stop reading for a moment and consider your *own* emotional status. Do you *know* what you are feeling at the moment or do you have to search around for words to describe what you are feeling. The person who can identify their feelings can experience them, own them and accept them as part of the human condition. It is possible to become increasingly aware of your emotional status merely by *choosing* to notice that status.

Acceptance

Once identification of emotional status has occurred, the next step is to *accept* it. The temptation (particularly when the emotion is a negative one) is for us to want our emotions to be other than they are. We often chide ourselves for feeling a certain way. It could be otherwise. We could, usefully, *accept* what we are feeling and thus further take responsibility for ourselves and for our emotions.

Control

We cannot always express our feelings as we experience them. The counsellor or helper, for example, who always cries when a client starts crying is unlikely to be able to support such clients for long: the whole process will become too emotionally exhausting. Instead, we can choose to *control* our feelings. That is not to say that we have to bottle them up indefinitely nor repress them. It is to acknowledge that we can *choose* when we express them. The important point, here, of course, is that we choose to express them *at some time*! The person who does not have positive emotional status often *believes* that he or she will discharge emotion at a later date but instead, bottles that emotion up or rationalises it in one of the ways suggested above. The skill in controlling emotion lies also in being able to discharge it later.

Redirection

Sometimes we cannot express emotion directly. We may, for example, be unaware of what the cause of our emotional state is. Or we may have angry feelings towards a person that we cannot express directly to them (a dead relative, for example). In these cases we can choose to redirect our emotion through another channel: artistic expression, creative work or vigorous competitive exercise. Thus the emotion is released in a harmless and yet gratifying way.

Switching

It is tempting to believe that our emotions have control over us. We sometimes prefer to believe that we cannot choose our emotions. Another point of view is that we can acknowledge and own our feelings and, if we so choose, *switch* those feelings to others. For example, we may acknowledge that we are angry and unsettled and accept that. We may then consciously switch from an angry unsettled state to a more placid one, having made a contract with ourselves to return to explore the angry state at a later date. Again, the emphasis is on making sure that we *do* return to explore the anger.

This switching of emotions takes time and skill. We first need to be able to identify and accept our feelings. Once we have done that we are nearer to being able to make the mental adjustment required to shift a gear into a different and more positive state. Such emotional switching is of considerable importance to counsellors or helpers who constantly work with emotionally distressed clients. In a way, many counsellors or helpers already practise switching without really thinking about it. The point is to make the practice a *conscious* one.

Transmutation

In transmutation, the emotion is not merely switched nor is it redirected. Instead it is changed by the person through an internal process that allows the emotion to seep away and to become something more positive. Meditation and prayer are both examples of how strong negative emotions can be subtly transmuted into more serene ones. Being able to 'step outside' of the emotion and being able to put it into a larger perspective can help too. For example, it is sometimes possible to identify a negative feeling and then to reflect on the status of that emotion in terms of one's entire life, or in terms of the entire world, or in terms of the whole history of the world: suddenly, the steam is taken out of the emotion and it can very quickly evaporate into laughter or bemusement at ever having invested so much energy in what turns out to be a small matter.

These are processes for dealing with emotions positively. Sometimes emotions *cannot* be dealt with in this way: they need expression. In the next section, methods are described to help the release of bottled-up emotion. They are best used by people in pairs: one person has the bottled-up emotion, the other is a colleague or friend who is prepared to help. Having said that, many of these methods can be adapted for use by the person working on his or her own. Once experience and familiarity has been gained in working with emotions in this way and once the person has become skilled in the *positive* use of emotion, as described above, he or she can continue to take charge of his or her own emotional status. The counsellor or helper who can identify, accept, express and redirect or transmute emotions in this way is increasing his or her emotional competence and is developing powerful ways of coping with stress. He or she is also more likely to be effective in helping his or her clients with their own emotional needs and wants. For one thing seems certain: we are unlikely to be able to help other people in their emotional upset if we, too, are unable to deal with our own feelings.

Counselling as micro-skills

There is considerable debate in the counselling literature – and in counselling teaching – as to whether or not counselling can be thought of as a set of 'skills' which can be learned. On the one hand, it certainly seems that there are certain practices that are going to help people and certain ones that are going to hinder their development. On the other hand, if we imagined that we could reduce the whole of counselling to a set of verbal and non-verbal skills, then we would probably be missing out on the 'human' side of the enterprise. For helping other people is never simply about using a particular expression or a certain tone of voice but also about entering into the way the other person feels. The problem is that the latter aspect of the relationship is probably much more difficult to describe (and thus to teach) than is the former. Perhaps a compromise, here, is to suggest that a starting point in learning about counselling might be to consider the skills involved and then to discuss, as those skills are being developed, how the human qualities of the counsellor enhance the counselling relationship.

The term 'micro-skills' is sometimes used when particular aspects of the counselling process are broken down into small chunks and practised on their own. Thus it is possible to acknowledge that asking 'open' questions (e.g. 'How do you feel about that?') are preferable, in many cases, to closed ones (e.g. 'And did that work?', 'Do you still care about him?'). Learning to discriminate and practise these micro-skills can form a platform from which the new counsellor works. But, as we have seen, it must go further than this. It is likely to be really important that the new counsellor does not begin to believe that all he or she has to do is to master these micro-skills and then go out into the world and use them with his or her clients.

Open and closed questions

It would appear, at first sight, that much of what a counsellor does is ask questions. This may or may not be true. It is my contention that the 'best' counselling takes place when the counsellor is able to be almost invisible in the relationship and has little, if anything, to say to the client. This is not out of a sense of inadequacy but out of a belief, perhaps, that, in the end, it is the client who finds his or her way out of his or her problems.

At least two types of basic question can be identified: the open and the closed question. The open question is the sort that the counsellor cannot have an answer to. It is a question that enables the client to elaborate and to say more. Often, these questions start with 'why', 'when', 'who', 'where' or 'how'. Examples of open questions are:

• How long have you felt like this?
• What did you do next?
• Who was involved, when that happened?
• How are you feeling at the moment?

Closed questions, on the other hand, are usually information-gathering questions and usually have a definite answer. Some may be answered by a straight 'yes' or 'no'. Examples of closed questions include:

• What are your children's names?
• You say you left school when you were 18?
• How old are you?

It is probably the case that open questions help the counselling session to move along and encourage the client to elaborate on his or her feelings and thoughts. However, closed questions can help to clarify particular points and help the counsellor to be clearer about the 'facts' of this person's life. Closed questions may be useful at the beginning of a counselling relationship to enable the counsellor to understand the broader picture behind the client's conversation. As the relationship develops, it seems likely that the counsellor will use fewer and fewer closed questions and more and more open ones.

There are more specific sorts of questions that are useful in counselling. These can be identified as follows.

Questions that seek examples

These are useful when people are talking in a general sort of way. Questions that seek examples enable both the client and the counsellor to become more specific. An illustration of this sort of question might be: 'Can you give me an example of when you felt like that?' This is often, usefully, followed up by inviting the client to describe the incident in more detail.

Questions that seek specifics

These are questions that home in on the elements of a particular situation or feeling. Examples, here, might include: 'what were the *particular* things that worried you about that situation?', 'in what particular ways did he upset you?', 'what was the very worst (or best) thing about that?'

Questions that seek to get to the nub of the situation

These sorts of questions are useful when talking to the person who 'overtalks' – who talks around a topic, offering considerable detail but seemingly avoiding getting to the nub of the issue. These are challenging questions: 'what do you *really* feel for this man?', 'if you could sum up you feelings in just a few words, what would they be?', 'given all that you have told me, do you still love him?'

Questions that help to form a plan

Sometimes in counselling and helping, the discussion can remain at an abstract level. Arguably, as we have seen throughout this book, the aim must be to encourage *action*. These sorts of questions help focus the client on what practical steps he or she is going to take to change the situation they find themselves in. Such questions can range from the broad: 'what do you want to do about all this?' to the staged: 'what is the first part of this that we can tackle?' It is often a good idea to help to break down problem resolution into small, manageable stages.

If the initial question is too 'large', then the client is likely to feel over-whelmed and unable to seek change. Change usually has to happen reasonably slowly, over time and with the help of manageable and achievable goals.

Imagining the future

Speculating about the future can be helpful if only in helping to clarify goals. Questions of this sort might include: 'what would things be like if you *did* split up?' or 'how would it be if you handed in your notice?' or 'what would happened if you *allowed* yourself to do that?'

Confronting questions

There is a wide range of these sorts of questions and they probably need to be used carefully and with tact. If they are used too often, they are seen as too confrontational. On the other hand, if confrontational questions are never used, the counselling or helping relationship can seem a little bland. Examples of confronting questions are as follows: 'ideally, what do you *really* want to do?', 'do you *have* to do this?', 'what would happen if you stopped doing this?'

There is one particular, slightly aberrant type of confronting question that is used by some counsellors and is aimed at getting beyond a certain resistance on the part of the client. It is a response to the answer to a counsellor's question, from the client: 'I don't know...'. The counsellor then asks the question 'what would the answer be if you *did* know?' Sometimes, this question elicits an interesting and thought-provoking answer. At other times, it simply results in the client saying 'I told you, I don't know!' There are mixed views on the degree to which this particular type of question is useful. Some counsellors use it fairly frequently while others see it as a form of intrusion.

The following example brings together some of these particular sorts of questions.

CLIENT: We have lived together for five years now and seem to row like mad over the simplest of things. I don't know...I still love him and the physical side of our relationship is good but we argue so much I wonder if it is worth our carrying on. When I am away, at work, I often find myself nearly crying when I think about what we used to be like together. And now it just seems to be reduced to...I don't know...nothing much, really.

COUNSELLOR: *Do* you still love him?

CLIENT: Yes! No...I don't know. I think I do but when we argue, sometimes, I just think: 'where's all this going? What are we doing to each other? What's the point?' But I know that if we split up, I'd only miss him.

COUNSELLOR: Would he miss you?

CLIENT: I know he would! He always says he couldn't manage without me. He's quite a dependent sort of person and he always reckons he'd be no good on his own.

COUNSELLOR: Imagine if everything was sorted out between you...what would that be like?

CLIENT: I would still feel the same about him....I'm pretty sure that I do love him. We wouldn't argue so much. We would share things more. I mean, one of the things we are always arguing about is how little he does around the place. He leaves an awful lot of it to me.

COUNSELLOR: So what's the first thing you have to do, here?

CLIENT: Talk to him, I suppose. Sit down and talk to him. We are so rushed, both of us, that we rarely have time to do that.

COUNSELLOR: Yet you have time to argue?

CLIENT: [LAUGHS] Yes, I see what you mean. We could set aside some time...

COUNSELLOR: And how will you do that? How will you organise it so that that happens?

CLIENT: Strike while the iron's hot, I guess! I'll talk to him about it tonight. He knows I come here.

COUNSELLOR: Talks about talks?

CLIENT: No, it's got to be more specific than that. I shall ring him at work and say that I want us to sit down, tonight, and talk.

COUNSELLOR: What is his response likely to be?

CLIENT: I don't know...

COUNSELLOR: And if you did know...?

CLIENT: He'll agree! I know he wants to sort this out. It can't be much of a life for him at the moment. I shall ring him when I leave here.

Reflection and selective reflection

A frequently identified micro-skill in the counselling literature is reflection – sometimes known as echoing. The task, here, is to help the client to continue to talk and to develop a particular line of thinking. Reflection is a technique that allows the counsellor or helper to encourage the client to continue talking, without that counsellor's own views getting in the way. The technique involves simply echoing back to the client the last few words spoken by him or her. Here is an example of reflection in action.

CLIENT: I started to feel things were going wrong when we moved to Brighton. I don't know...my husband started to get sort of distant...

COUNSELLOR: Your husband started to get distant...

CLIENT: He didn't seem to want to talk very much or discuss things any more. We became detached from each other. We used to share so much and then, suddenly, he had other interests...

COUNSELLOR: Other interests...

CLIENT: Yes. We used to share the same interests, do things together and then, suddenly, there was nothing...

There are some points to be made about this skill. First, it needs to be done discretely and carefully. If it is overused, or used clumsily, it becomes very visible to the client. It can also sound remarkably like parroting and simply reflecting for the sake of reflecting. Second, the tone of voice used by the client should also be echoed by the counsellor and the reflection should not turn into a question. If we consider the fragment cited above, with the reflection becoming a question, we can see what may happen.

CLIENT: I started to feel things were going wrong when we moved to Brighton. I don't know...my husband started to get sort of distant...

COUNSELLOR: Your husband started to get sort of distant?

CLIENT: Yes!

The result, as we see, can be an abrupt and closed answer to a direct question. Reflection, then, is not another form of questioning but a gentle attempt at helping the client to continue their narrative.

Selective reflection is related to straight reflection but also differs from it. It is the lifting of a piece of speech that has been emphasised by the client and which is repeated back by the counsellor. Here is an example of selective reflection.

CLIENT: We lived, for awhile with my husband's sister. I hated her! I really couldn't bear being in the same room. Anyway, we seem to manage for a few months until we were able to find another flat.

COUNSELLOR: You hated your husband's sister...

CLIENT: I completely hated her. I sensed that she thought that she and my husband were much closer to each other than *we* were. She came to represent everything I loathe in people...

In this example, what is reflected back is not the very last thing that is said by the client but the section that has been emphasised by her. It may be thought that some people talk in such a monotone as never to emphasise particular parts of what they say. However, closer listening to clients illustrates that we all, at times, emphasise particular points and that selective reflection is not so difficult as it may at first appear.

Empathy building

Empathy building involves the counsellor or helper indicating to the client that he or she is really understood. This can be conveyed by short expressions that indicate that the client has appropriately understood the feelings being conveyed by the client. If the counsellor gets it right, it can help the counselling relationship along. If the counsellor gets it wrong, it is important that he or she backs away a little and pays more attention to listening to the client. Here are two examples: one in which empathy building works, the other in which it does not.

CLIENT: I felt that everything just wasn't working out. I felt sort of mixed up about my relationship with Danny. I didn't know what he wanted of me. He seemed to be asking too much. I don't know, I sort of felt upset and...I couldn't understand him.
COUNSELLOR: You felt angry with him?
CLIENT: Yes! I was mad with him – mad at him! I wanted to hit him at one stage.

CLIENT: We talked a lot about what would happen if we split up. I wanted to know how she felt if she did. What would happen between us: what would happen to the kids and everything. She said she didn't know....I suppose neither of us knew, really...
COUNSELLOR: You felt lost...
CLIENT: No, not at all! We were certain about what we wanted to do, in one way. We knew that we couldn't go on as we were. We knew, I suppose that we would break up. It was just a question of working out the ins and outs of it.

Empathy building needs to be used sensitively and, perhaps, only occasionally. Like reflection, it can be over-used and become obvious. The counsellor always runs the risk of being seen by the client as exercising a set of skills that he or she wields according to the situation. The best sort of counselling, though, is that which is fairly spontaneous and seamless: it occurs when neither the counsellor nor the client is particularly aware of what skills the counsellor is using. And herein lies a paradox. On the one hand, the counsellor needs to learn certain skills. On the other, they must be invisible. It seems likely that these things occur in stages. At first, when learning the skills, the counsellor is less than subtle. As he or she gains experience in using the skills and internalises them, they become more and more part of the person, they become more and more invisible.

Summarising

Summarising is where the counsellor sums up a longish piece of talk by the client and tries to identify the key issues. There is always a danger, here, that what the counsellor identifies as 'the issues' may not, necessarily be the same as those perceived by the client. However, the client is likely to note any incongruities in the counsellor's summarising and correct them or add to them. Here is an example of summarising.

CLIENT: We spend an awful long time working out how we were going to live together. You know, the nuts and bolts of things. We talked about how we would get the flat set up. What we would tell our parents. What would happen when we really talked to them about being gay. Whether or not we should have told them a long time ago. In a way, we were asking a lot of them. We were both coming out to our parents at the same time: plus we were breaking it to them that we were going to live together. There was no way of knowing how either set of parents would take all that. I thought that mine might be OK – although I wasn't sure about my parents. Martin had some doubts that either of his parents would like it. I say 'like it', that's a bit of an understatement. He thought that they would go barmy! Might throw him out. And then he would have no one to go back to, if things didn't work out between me and him. Not that we thought, at that stage, that they wouldn't.

COUNSELLOR: Let me just try to focus a bit on what you are saying. You felt that you had to get the way you lived together sorted out and that part of that involved you both coming out to your parents. And you were less than sure how your parents would take that.

CLIENT: And, particularly, how Martin would cope if his parents hit the roof. It's funny, but even at that stage, we talked about 'what would happen if we broke up'. It seems ironic, now.

Checking for understanding

Conversation, like thinking, is not necessarily a linear process. We do not always convey our thoughts to another person in a logical, rational stream. Sometimes, the counselling conversation, on the part of the client, can become slightly confusing. At times, this may not matter. It is sometimes important to let people talk freely and easily and to pay more attention to the process that is occurring rather than becoming obsessed by the meaning of what the other person is saying. At other times, though, it is important to clarify, to try to pin the client down to what he or she means by what he or she is saying.

CLIENT: It goes a long way back. I suppose I always knew that something was up. She used to come home after work and, I don't know, she sort of seemed non-committal. She was just the same in many ways but things were different. It wasn't anything she said, just a sort of atmosphere. We talked easily enough about things and... you know, we had meals together and sat down and watched the box.

COUNSELLOR: Let me see if I have grasped what you are saying. You felt there was something wrong between you – although it was difficult to say exactly what it was?

CLIENT: Something like that. If I am honest, I suppose my feelings for her were changing but what was coming over, when we talked, was that she had someone else....It turned out that she did.

Closure

The term *closure* is sometimes applied to the resolution of a problem. The idea is that we worry about problems until we find a way of rationalising them and putting them into the past. Part of the counsellor or helper's role is to help the other person to reach a reasonable degree of closure with regard to the issues that concern them. On the other hand, life may not be quite as simple as this. Although we have to find ways of living with the life situations we have been through, the idea that we can somehow wrap them up and clear them away may be something of a fallacy. Perhaps the most we can hope for is a relative degree of closure: to the point where we can continue to function reasonably well without having 'forgotten', entirely, the things we have worried about.

The term 'premature closure' is sometimes applied to a situation where a person only partially resolves a problem but 'files it away' before it is fully worked through. In this case, the theory goes, the problem is not resolved but survives, in the background, and continues to nag away at the person. Sometimes, trying to be too 'tidy' as a counsellor or helper can cause this premature closure. In the rush to help, the helper forces the other person to jump to an easy way of dealing with a problem. What appears to be a resolution is simply the client's attempt at pleasing the counsellor or helper.

Much may depend on the counsellor's own experience of dealing with problems. If he or she tends to find it easy to let problems go and to let them slip into the past, he or she may, unwittingly, encourage the client to do the same. As we have noted elsewhere, this is a case of the counsellor's not assuming that the person that he or she is helping operates in exactly the same way as the counsellor. The client's problems are not the counsellor's and vice versa. Nor are the client's ways of resolving problems necessarily those that the counsellor uses in his or her own life. While certain life problems may seem universal, the ways of coping with them are not. This may, indeed, be a basic assumption of the counselling process. We run into problems as counsellors and helpers when we begin to blur the distinction between our own ways of operating and the operating procedures of those whom we are trying to help. Once again, we need to be able to at least try to enter the frame of reference of the other person – the 'life world' of the other.

Learning basic strategies

Although learning about counselling is discussed in more detail in the final chapter of this book, it is worth noting, at this point, that various options are open to the person who wants to learn to be more effective either as a counsellor or as a person who uses counselling skills. First, they may complete a formal counselling course. A certificate course normally lasts between one and two years and a diploma course two or three years. Most counselling courses teach both the theory and practice of counselling although some focus on one or the other and it is important to clarify, before starting the course, which applies. Second, they may learn the skills through courses set within modules in health-care courses. Many training courses in the health-care professions offer modules in counselling and/or counselling skills. Finally, a person may choose to be self-taught by practising the skills, intentionally, while working with clients. The latter route, by some, may be seen as the least responsible. However, many of the activities we undertake in life are learned, experientially, by doing. The same may or may not apply to basic counselling skills.

Confidentiality

The issue of confidentiality in counselling is a complex one. Should one, for instance, offer total confidentiality to a client, whatever the circumstances? Is it reasonable to say to a potential client that nothing that is discussed between you will be discussed in any other forum?

We may tackle the problem by considering some specific examples. Supposing, for instance, that we offer total confidentially in the relationship. Imagine, then, that during a counselling conversation, the client discloses strong suicidal feelings. Do we then maintain the total confidentiality that we have offered or argue that this particular circumstance somehow overides the original contract we had with the client? Similarly, if we are working as a counsellor in a college and have offered complete confidentiality to a student in counselling, who, subsequently suggests that a lecturer has indecently assaulted her, do we break the confidentiality contract that we have with that student?

The answers, in both cases, might vary according to the view you take of the importance of confidentiality. After all, the Samaritan organisation, in the UK, offers totally confidentiality to all its telephone clients and claims that this is part of what makes the service work. However, most 'independent' counsellors and helpers are either working within a profession or are working as private counsellors. Neither are particularly likely to have the considerable back-up service that the Samaritan organisation is able to offer.

It is my view that offering total confidentiality is not a particularly good idea – except, paradoxically, *in extremis*. That is to say that the general rule might be that we do not offer total confidentiality except if it is clear that this person at this time needs, desperately, to talk to someone and will only do so if total confidentiality is offered. In this case, it would seem to be less than human to do otherwise – regardless of what the person is about to disclose.

The 'not offering total confidentiality' issue is also a fairly thorny issue but one that can be discussed. One option is not to discuss the confidentiality issue unless it is raised by the client. This would seem to be a little disingenuous and may cause problems later in the relationship if the question of confidentiality is raised then. It would be hard to say, at a later date, the equivalent of 'as we haven't discussed confidentiality in the past, I can't promise to maintain it now'. Another option is to offer confidentiality, generally, but that we would reserve the right to renegotiate that confidentiality, in certain circumstances, if future events require that this happens. An example of this would be that for the most part everything the client says to us is held in confidence. However, if an issue such as abuse by a relative or a teacher arose in the counselling relationshp, we would be prepared to invite the client to allow us to disclose certain facts to another party. The problem arises, here, if the client decides that we should *not* disclose certain facts to another party. This would, for example, present us with very considerable responsibility if the client disclosed that he or she was suicidal but refused to allow us to tell another person.

A further option would be the 'confidentiality in most circumstances, except if either the client or the counsellor felt that it was imperative to tell another person'. This is clumsy but it covers a range of issues, including the situations outlined above. It allows both the client *and* the counsellor to exercise some rights relating to confidentiality.

Whatever option is chosen, it is important for all counsellors to have their own policy about confidentiality and to make sure that it is explicated clearly to the clients that they counsel or help. Clearly, there are occasions when, during informal or brief counselling, the issue of confidentiality need not be raised but it seems likely that it always should be if counselling is to continue over any length of time.

Organising the counselling relationship

The idea of organisation, in this context, may sound something of an anathema to some people. However, given that most of us are limited by time and resources, it seems useful to bring some sort of structure to bear when trying to help others. Also, many people who would be counsellors find themselves stuck at various points and wonder 'what should I be doing now?' The following structure is by no means set in stone and individual relationships will produce their own structures. However, this one does give a starting point to thinking about what to do and when.

- Introductions: self and other
- Letting the person tell their story
- Identifying problem areas
- Prioritising
- Working through the problems

- Practising in the real world
- Reviewing progress and identifying new goals
- Re-gaining independence
- Concluding the relationship.

Introductions: self and other

The way in which two people introduce themselves is probably quite important. During this stage, you establish how you like to be addressed (first name, surname, nickname and so on). You are also sizing each other up a little and trying to make sense of whether or not you are likely to be able to help this person. Similarly, they are trying to work out whether or not they can trust you to tell you their story and talk through their problems.

At this point, too, you need to develop an 'opener', a way of letting the person start to talk to you. My tendency is to ask, directly, 'how can I help?' There is a range of other possibilities, including, at least: 'what is it that brings you here today?', 'what would you like to talk about?', 'how do you think I can help you?' Whatever opener you use, you should consider practising it and refining it until it becomes part of yourself. This is not to say that it should sound over-rehearsed or automatic but simply that, like a personal greeting, both parties will feel more comfortable if the opener sounds natural and fits the occasion.

Letting the person tell their story

After the introduction, it is often useful if the other person is allowed simply to tell you about themselves. This is not a formal, history-taking session but a chance for the counsellor to hear about the other person's background. It is often out of this story that current problems emerge and certainly the background offers the context for the present problems.

Identifying problem areas

In this stage, the counsellor and client begin to identify problem areas. I write 'problem areas' because I feel that it is important that the counsellor does not spring too quickly to identify specific problems. Various possibilities arise out of this idea. First, the client may come to the counsellor with very specific problems in mind about which he or she wants to talk. However, during that talking, it often emerges that the previously identified problems are not the only ones and that others trickle to the surface. Alternatively, a person may come to a counsellor or helper without really being clear about what their problems are but simply being aware of feeling very uncomfortable or anxious. Thus it is important to explore problem areas slowly and carefully and to try to establish what are 'really' problems and what are issues slightly to one side of those problems.

It is important, too, for the counsellor to bear in mind the principle that the client's problems are not the counsellor's and the counsellor's are not the client's. It is easy for us to imagine that the things that bother us are the things that bother other people and this often turns out not to be the case. We should, perhaps, meet each client as a 'blank slate' and make no assumptions about what is or what is not a problem in this particular person's case.

Prioritising

Once certain core problems have been identified, they can be prioritised. What, for example, is the issue that is most pressing, that needs to be dealt with most immediately? What problems will be resolved through the resolution of other problems? What are the most *practical* issues that need to be dealt with? In my experience, it is often better to deal with the practical, life issues that *can* be dealt with, first, leaving the more 'psychological' problems until later. Often, dealing with the practical problems can help in the resolution of the psychological.

Working through the problems

In this stage, client and counsellor work out a plan for dealing with the problems that have emerged. 'Dealing with' is, perhaps, too large a concept. Some problems, clearly, have to be lived with. Counselling can never sort out all of the societally determined problems that face most people during the course of their lives. Again, it is important to work on those issues that *can* be worked on. The others may be a question of working out strategies for living with.

Practising in the real world

Counselling is nothing if *action* does not follow from it. I cannot believe that simply talking about things changes them. There must also be a change in the person's life – even if that is a very slight change. The 'practising in the real world' stage is where the client goes away from the counsellor and sees how what they have both talked about relates to the real world of daily living. There are usually false starts and disappointments in this phase. It is sometimes much easier to clarify things at a theoretical level, during conversation, than it is to convert that talk into action. It is here that the counsellor will act in a supporting role and be prepared to occasionally have to pick the client up and start again.

Reviewing progress and identifying new goals

This is a continuous process, throughout the counselling relationship. The client and counsellor review what they have decided to do in the real world and check that against what they have talked about. Eventually, it becomes clear that some things that have been talked about work and others have to be reformulated or allowed to fall by the wayside. Counselling is not a scientific process and assessing what is best for any given person (either by themselves or in conversation with the counsellor) can be very much a hit-and-miss affair. Often, both counsellor and client have to live with compromise.

Re-gaining independence

Gradually, the counselling relationship increasingly becomes driven by the client. It will be the client who makes more and more suggestions about how he or she should and wants to live and the client who tries out more and more experiments with making changes. During this time, there is a gradual moving away from the counsellor by the client. This, in turn, leads to the conclusion of the relationship.

Concluding the relationship

Finishing a counselling relationship is not always easy. Both parties have invested a good deal in the relationship. Further, the client, having grown independent, may not always *thank* the counsellor. And this is appropriate, for, as we have noted, it is the client who 'does the work' in the relationship and who, in the end, brings about the changes. However, it is only human to expect that a counsellor who has been with a client for some considerable time may feel a little hurt if the client does not thank them in some way. Growing used to this possibility may be part of the maturation process of the counsellor. The counsellor is, in a way, constantly trying to work himself or herself out of a job. And once he or she achieves that goal, he or she should be pleased that it has happened – at least, in theory!

A question mark hangs over whether or not the counsellor should offer to leave the door open to the client and allow him or her to return should they feel the need. One school of thought is of the view that this fosters further dependence, another is of the view that it is human to allow a fall-back position if it is found to be necessary. Perhaps each counsellor has to determine this issue for himself or herself and perhaps may have different rules for different clients.

6 Handling difficult situations

Sometimes, counselling and helping go smoothly: the client is able to talk through problems, identify solutions and a natural end to the relationships occurs. Sometimes, however, things do not go as smoothly as this. In this chapter, various difficult situations are described and possible solutions identified. Much, in the end, will be dependent upon the context of the difficult situations. Like counselling, itself, it is rarely possible to offer fail-safe solutions and the experienced counsellor and helper learns his or her own set of coping strategies. Above all, perhaps, he or she identifies what must be ethical positions in relation to problems. For counselling, whatever it is not, must be an ethical endeavour.

Romantic and sexual attraction

It is not particularly uncommon for people who are involved in a counselling or helping relationship to find themselves attracted to each other. Sometimes, this attraction is reciprocal and sometimes it is not. Either way, the situation needs to be faced and ways of dealing with it addressed. It is neither ethical nor, usually, particularly helpful to client or counsellor to act on the feelings that emerge at this level. Unfortunately, this also means that the counsellor carries the responsibility for identifying that a romantic or sexual attraction is occurring. If we were all perfect at what we did, then we could, presumably, just note the fact and do something about it. As we are not perfect, it may be some time before we can be honest with ourselves (and perhaps with our clients) over these issues.

The psychodynamic practitioner often sees attraction of these sorts in terms of *transference*. Transference is said to occur when the client begins to view the counsellor as the ideal person to help – perhaps seeing the counsellor as the ideal mother or father that he or she never had. As a result of this transference, the feelings experienced by the client for the counsellor can be intense. Counter-transference is said to occur when similar (or, sometimes, opposite) feelings are stimulated in the counsellor. In classical psychoanalysis, analysis is said to be complete when the transference situation is resolved.

On another level, however, it seems reasonable to expect that two people who talk to each other about very personal or even intimate things may become attracted to each other. After all, this mimics, almost exactly, how ordinary friendships, away from counselling, develop into loving relationships. The question, in counselling, is how best the situation may be handled.

At a risk of being dogmatic, I think it is important to state that first, the counsellor must take responsibility for the nature of the relationships and that second, the counsellor has an ethical duty not to exploit the relationship in any way. It should be borne in mind that the romantic and/or sexual feelings experienced by the client for the counsellor are not occurring under 'normal' circumstances but are determined, to some degree at least, by the *nature* of the counselling relationship. If that relationship were to be normalised and the counsellor and client simply became friends and not counsellor and client, it seems reasonable to assume that the dynamics of the relationship may change. The question is, what is the counsellor to do?

First, the counsellor must be honest about his or her own feelings. As we have noted, this is often the most difficult part. He or she must acknowledge, to himself or herself in the first instance, that romantic or sexual feelings are present. If they are present on the part of the counsellor for the client and are not obviously being reciprocated by the client, then the counsellor may choose to work these issues through with a supervisor. Another option is to gently suggest to the client that they see another counsellor – although it is fully acknowledged that such an option may not be, practically, a particularly easy or pain-free one to set up. Alternatively, the counsellor, if he or she feels themselves to be 'strong' enough, may choose to continue the relationship whilst not, on any account, exploiting the feelings of the client. However, this assumes that such a 'strong' person has complete control over his or her feelings and this may or may not be the case. Whatever decision is made, there would never seem to be the option of *acting* on romantic or sexual feelings with the client.

A much more debatable option is whether or not the counsellor discusses his or her feelings with the client. At its worst, this may place an unbearable strain on both the client and the relationship. Also, there is a slight danger that the client will feel forced to reciprocate feelings that are not 'really' present.

When the feelings between client and counsellor are reciprocal, the relationship has the potential to be even more difficult to manage. It is advised that, in this situation, the counsellor does seek out a supervisor – if only on a temporary basis – with whom to discuss the situation. It is arguable that a counsellor who 'allows' a reciprocal relationship of this sort to develop is not sufficiently experienced or clear about his or her own boundaries in a therapeutic relationship. On the other hand, humans, being what they are, can never really account for how relationships will develop and even the most experienced counsellor is likely to be confronted at some stage with unexpected feelings.

There are, of course, a range of different possibilities in this area. It is quite possible, for instance, that the heterosexual client will find himself or herself attracted to the homosexual counsellor or vice versa. In this case, depending on the feelings of each party about their own sexuality, a new set of dynamics may come into play. If the counsellor has not worked through his or her own feelings about sexual orientation, then he or she may find himself or herself confused, defensive or even offended – as may the client in a similar situation. It may or may not be possible to talk these issues through as part of the counselling relationship but it should by no means be taken for granted that somehow this cross-orientation relationship will be 'easier' to handle that a heterosexual–heterosexual or homosexual–homosexual one. Occasionally, too, the counselling relationship will be one in which orientations will be 'discovered' by the counsellor or the client: the counsellor may suddenly be surprised by a strength of feeling for a same-sex client – as may a client. Again, for the counsellor, this may be a point at which a considerable amount of supervision may be called for and it may be a 'growth point' for the counsellor who, previously, had not been aware of a facet of his or her sexuality. It should be noted that there is an increasing tendency, in the literature on sexuality, to discuss the idea of people having 'sexualties' rather than 'a sexuality'.

Despite all the injunctions to keep the counsellor–client relationship on a strictly professional level, it seems likely that, occasionally, emotional relationships will develop that are long lasting. In this case, it seems best to advise that the counselling relationship between the pair be terminated. It seems difficult to argue that a couple who are now enjoying an independent, emotional relationship can maintain the sort of counselling relationship that has gone before. In the end, we are unlikely to be the best counsellors for our life partners.

Breaking bad news

Bad news can come in various forms. For those in the health professions, the tendency will be for the idea of bad news to immediately be associated with life-threatening illness or the death of a family or group member. However, there are degrees of bad news, ranging from the break-up of a relationship and the realisation that a relationship will never be the same through to the fact that death, for this person, is unlikely to be far away. Many people shy away from talking about bad news because they find it difficult to know how *they* will react after they have broken it. For most of us, I suspect, breaking bad news is one of the most difficult interpersonal situations we have to face.

There are no hard-and-fast rules here. Much depends on the context, the people involved and the strength of the relationship that exists between the person bearing the news and the receiver. Indeed, there may be some advantage to having a person who is not intimately related to the client being the breaker of bad news. This is, of course, a situation often faced by the police when they have to visit people's houses after fatal accidents or when critical injury has occurred. The fact that the police have no vested or personal interest in the situation may or may not make it easier to bear.

The 'sandwich' approach is sometimes advocated in breaking bad news. This is a three-stage model, as follows, and it sounds a little bleak when written out on the page. However, it can help as a guide-line to thinking about the way to handle the breaking of bad news.

Stage 1 The bearer tells the person that they have bad news to break.
Stage 2 This is *immediately* followed by the bad news, itself, spoken in unequivocal terms.
Stage 3 The bearer remains with the person to offer quiet support.

The idea of stage 1 is that it prepares the hearer for a shock. It allows them to sit down, if necessary, and to steel themselves for what is to come. No one likes bad news blurted out almost as an aside or mentioned along with other issues. It needs to be made clear that what is to follow is important and needs to be listened to.

In stage 2, the bearer of the news tells it as clearly and with as little ambiguity as possible. It is really important that no false hope is offered here and that the listener really hears and understands what is being said. It is probably best, when reporting death, for example, to avoid euphemisms such as 'slipped away' or 'passed over' and better, perhaps, to use the word 'died'. Despite using the clearest language, it is quite possible that the hearer will *not* hear what is being said and that the speaker may have to ascertain that what he or she has said has been taken in. Faced with truly shocking news, many of us exhibit the ability to cut ourselves off from it and deny it. In these cases, there is an argument for the talker to go back over what has been said and repeat it as necessary.

It is also important, at this time, that the breaker of the news does not *overtalk*. We often have a tendency to overtalk when we are anxious or, paradoxically, when we are not clear what we should be saying. At such times, it may seem better to say something than to say nothing. However, in stage 3 of this model, it may be more useful to the hearer if the talker then stays quiet, allows the news to sink in and is 'available' for the other person. The hearer of the bad news may react in any number of ways. There may be tears or there may not. The person may get angry or, as we have seen, deny what he or she has heard. Sometimes, the news is heard with blank indifference or matter of factness. Some people do not need support immediately after they have heard bad news but days or even weeks later when it has had time to sink in. One of the problems of the 'counsellors were standing by' syndrome after major disasters may well be that counselling is being offered too soon. We do not always want to talk things through immediately after we have heard bad news or had something awful happen to us. We may, however, need quite considerable support some time later.

What the counsellor has to do in stage 3 is to try and gauge what it is that the hearer of the news is asking of him or her. Sometimes, this can take the direct form of 'what would you like us to do?' and to act on the answer. Sometimes, the counsellor must read the situation and respond intuitively. Again, however, the important thing is not to overtalk and, sometimes, being engaged in some sort of physical activity can help: taking a walk, visiting relatives and so on. A frequent reaction during this phase is that the hearer may not be at all clear *what* they want or need and, again, patience and tact need to be exercised. There may be occasions when, temporarily, the counsellor has to 'take over' the client and make some concrete decisions for him or her. Such decisions can involve where that person spends the night, who else is contacted and so forth. Better, though, perhaps, that – wherever possible – the client makes these decisions. In the end, though, the skilled counsellor will 'listen' to what the hearer is asking for (or *not* asking for) and respond accordingly. Breaking bad news, however often it is done, can never become routine and thus there are no routines that fit every situation and every type of person. The three-stage model offered here can help to pave the way but, in the end, the counsellor has to accept, for himself or herself, the difficulty of the situation and the inevitable pain that will occur.

Working with problems that stimulate your own problems

Sometimes, in counselling, the client will begin to talk about problems that have echoes for the counsellor. The client will begin to describe situations, thoughts or feelings that are shared by the counsellor. The most difficult of these will be those that the counsellor has not yet faced up to. This, of itself, is a good argument for the practising counsellor to either engage in therapy or counselling themselves or to make sure that he or she has supervision as described in a previous chapter.

Stimulation of our own problems can arise gradually, as a theme of a conversation develops or, more alarmingly, very suddenly, as the client states something that he or she has been unable to articulate until that moment. In the first case, the counsellor has some time to prepare themselves for their reaction. Not that this, necessarily, makes the situation easier to deal with. However, when a sudden confrontation with the counsellor's own problems occurs, it seems likely that the counsellor will not be ready at all. Both of these situations often lead to similar sorts of reactions in the counsellor. That counsellor will begin to feel uncomfortable, may colour a little, may find that his or her voice becomes a little hoarse and finds himself or herself distracted by inner thoughts and feelings.

This, clearly, is not the time or the place for the counsellor to try to work out his or her own problems in the area. Such restimulation can be taken by the counsellor as a sign that, some time soon, he or she will have to do some work on exploring these problem areas within himself or herself. The question is, how does the counsellor face the situation *as it arises*?

There are various possibilities. One is for the counsellor to listen and allow the client to continue to talk about the stimulating issues but make few interventions. Thus the client becomes the main talker in the relationship at that time and the counsellor merely acts to help the person verbalise the problems. Another possibility is for the counsellor to move the client away from the area, very gently, with the view to exploring it at a later date when, he or she – the counsellor – has had time to talk the issue through with a supervisor and explore some of his or her own feelings about the issue. Whilst this may seem a practical solution, it may make the client feel that there are 'no-go' areas of conversation and even reinforce the idea that what he or she is talking about should not be talked about. Tact and resourcefulness are required here as the counsellor is dealing with two sets of awkward feelings: those of the client and his or her own feelings.

A third option, and a difficult one, is self-disclosure on the part of the counsellor. Here, the counsellor, without wanting to overwhelm the client, tells him or her that these problems are shared by the counsellor. This is something of a gamble. On the one hand, the client may feel relief that this person in front of them is also human and prone to the same sorts of difficulties. On the other, it may change the balance of the relationship and make the client feel some responsibility for 'helping' the counsellor. Further, the client may feel, 'if this counsellor cannot cope with these feelings in himself or herself, what chance have I got?' Again, much will depend on context and on the counsellor's prior knowledge of how the client is likely to react.

Whatever method is chosen to deal with the stimulation or restimulation, as it occurs, it seems reasonable to suggest that the counsellor *must* do something about the stimulation that has occurred. Simply to acknowledge it and move on, is not enough. Problems stimulated by client talk, in this way, are unlikely simply to go away and it is part of the counsellor's responsibility to go away and work through these problems.

The other point that needs to be made, here, is that the counsellor should not exploit the situation, in a voyeuristic way. There can sometimes be a tendency in us to feel that 'these are my problems too: I wonder what *this* person does about them?' or even to be excited by the prospect of talking about 'danger areas' in another person. Neither of these positions, however, is taking into account the counsellor's responsibility, first and foremost, to care for the client and to ensure that the client remains the focus of the relationship. Simply to encourage the client to talk as a means of seeking one's own salvation or out of vicarious interest, is unlikely to be helpful to the client. I suspect, too, that, at some level, the client becomes aware that this sort of exploitation is going on when it occurs. We cannot, in the end, hide our feelings all that well – especially when deeper and more difficult feelings are the basis of that particular conversation.

Personality differences

What, exactly, constitutes a personality difference between two people is difficult to define. Sometimes, it occurs because the two people are too similar to each other and each projects an image of themselves, on the other, and 'sees' themselves being mirrored back. Often, too, in similar people, it is the qualities that they do not like that stand out between them. Alternatively, sometimes two people do not get on because they are too different: there is little meeting ground between them. At other times, one person finds the other difficult because of his or her mannerisms, ways of speaking, their vocabulary and so on. It is any of these situations (and probably many more) that we tend to call personality differences and they can occur in counselling. It is usually easier for the counsellor if it is he or she that identifies the problem. We are often blind to another person finding *us* difficult to get on with. One useful idea is, in the early stages of the counselling relationship, to take time out to explore how each of you is getting on with the other. This is a type of evaluation of the counselling relationship. Here, the counsellor makes a particular decision to talk to the client about how each of them views the other. Although, on paper, this can sound contrived, in practice, it can prove to be an invaluable way of identifying whether both parties are working well with each other and, conversely, in highlighting personality differences. Although, as can be imagined, it is unlikely that the client will say, outright, that he or she finds the counsellor loathsome! The sensitive counsellor, however, should be able to assess the degree to which things are working out between the two.

How, then, to resolve the issue of a personality clash occurring between counsellor and client? One approach is to work through it. If we accept the idea that there is something that the client sees in the counsellor (or vice versa) that reminds him or her of a negative or disliked quality in themselves, it seems possible, in theory, to get to talking about these qualities. In practice, though, it takes a particularly skilled and self-aware counsellor to be able to help the client to verbalise such feelings. It also takes a certain stoicism on the part of the counsellor to sit and hear the sorts of issues being described. After all, in one sense, the client is describing what he or she sees in the counsellor and the picture may not be a very attractive one.

An alternative, is to suggest that, if the personality difference persists over time, the client is referred to another counsellor. This sort of issue can be dealt with right at the beginning of the relationship by the introduction, by the counsellor, of a clause allowing the client to suggest, at any time, if he or she would like to discontinue the relationship. Similarly, but with perhaps a little more difficulty, the counsellor may want to devise a similar clause at the beginning of the relationship by which he or she, the counsellor, can choose to discontinue the relationship should that prove in the best interest of the client. The question is, of course, when such a clause is brought into play – and who should decide? Probably, as with many of these sorts of issues, there is a gradual realisation that the counselling relationship is not working. As this becomes apparent, it seems likely that *either* the counsellor or the client will raise the issue of termination and referral. If not, then, again, it would seem reasonable that the counsellor raises the issue – at least tentatively – given that the client may feel nervous about doing so. The breaking up of a relationship in this way is rarely so easy. As with all similar partings – relationship breakdown, divorce, the discontinuation of a student–tutor relationship – there is likely to be some pain experienced by both parties and the counsellor may want to spend time, afterwards, reflecting on what this sort of separation has meant to him or her and what he or she can learn from it. He or she may also want to *allow* himself or herself some negative feelings about the client and not engage in too much self-flagellation over the issue. In the end, we cannot get on with everyone.

Getting bored

One of the difficulties of helping and counselling others is that some problems can recur frequently over time and with different people. Further, some clients prefer to *talk* about their problems rather than risk *doing* anything about them. Finally, in this short list of problems, any counsellor who is counselling on a regular basis is having to cope with people's woes and worries over a lengthy period of time. It is not surprising that, occasionally, it is possible to get bored in the process. This seems to be an issue that is often ignored in the literature or turned into a highly problematic construct. It seems to me that, at some point, we are *bound* to get bored in our dealings with others.

Part of the solution to this problem lies, perhaps, in making sure that one's own life, away from counselling, is personally fulfilling. This sort of advice can be levelled at anyone who finds their jobs boring – and there are of course many jobs far more boring than counselling and helping. Another alternative is to limit the hours that one engages in counselling and make sure that a reasonable balance is struck between counselling and engaging in other tasks. This may be relatively easy for the volunteer counsellor or for the person for whom counselling is only part of their role. It will not be so easy for the full-time, professional counsellor.

A third option is to accept periods of boredom and to appreciate that most of us have to work, occasionally, on 'automatic pilot'. The plain fact is that we cannot all give 100 per cent of ourselves, all of the time. There will be periods in our lives where we are much more effective as counsellors and helpers and periods where we are not. It seems impractical and unnecessary to berate ourselves too hard over this issue. It is probably reasonable to accept that we can be 'good enough' counsellors for a fair percentage of the time.

7   Looking after yourself

Counselling is a stressful activity. Listening to people's problems and then keeping those problems to yourself is not an easy task. It is essential, then, that we learn to look after ourselves as counsellors and helpers.

Self-help

There is much we can do to help ourselves. First, it is probably wise to limit the amount of counselling we do. While this may not be so easy if we are paid, full-time counsellors or helpers, it is easier if we are volunteers and choose to do the work. This may also mean learning to say 'no' to people and restricting access to yourself. No-one should expect you to be available 100 per cent of the time. This idea also extends to the question of whether or not you should allow clients to have your home phone number. My view on this is quite clear: I do not let clients (or students) have my home phone number at all. My feeling is that the time I have at home is 'my' time and is best spent with my family and friends and – myself. I know that if I have to talk to someone, on the phone, while at home, I do not give my full attention to them and that I also feel slightly resentful that the other person is taking advantage of my own free time. There are, of course, exceptions to this. Emergency situations, where a person feels suicidal, of course, may mean that they track down your phone number as a last resort. In this case, the general principle of protecting your own privacy is overridden by the principle of trying to help someone stay alive.

It is important, too, that counselling and helping are not the only activities we engage in. As with most jobs, it is important to consider *why* you choose to take part in this activity at all. Sometimes, the answer will be 'because it helps me to sort myself out'. If this is the primary motive, then it may not be a good one. If we seek our own salvation out of helping others, we may find that our ability to help is limited. It may be better to withdraw from the activities of counselling and helping and seek one's own help through therapy rather than seeking a solution to life's problems through listening to those of others. On the other hand, of course, it remains true that sometimes hearing about other people's problems and their solutions really does help us. But this is different to our seeking to clarify our lives through the problems of others.

Another form of self-help is to join a support group. Many people feel that it is important for counsellors and helpers to continue their own 'personal development' while they are acting as counsellors – although it may be said that exactly what 'personal development' is varies according to the books you read and the people you talk to. Some find it helpful to continue to talk through their own life experiences, in a group, to explore new life options and to reflect on their own feelings and thoughts on a regular basis. For some, personal development may also mean further educational or artistic development. It is not unreasonable to recommend that, for some, continuing education or the development of interests in theatre, music and art may be as important to a counsellor as other forms of self-development. Co-counselling offers, for some, another route to self-help.

Co-counselling

Co-counselling is a two-way process in which two people take it in turns to spend time as 'counsellor' and 'client'. The client takes time to verbalise and talk through issues and problems from everyday life, while the counsellor gives her attention. The counsellor in this relationship does not act in the traditional counselling manner. In other words, she does not offer advice nor attempt to 'sort out' the client. In this self-directed approach, the client herself learns to examine her own problems and to 'counsel herself'. Each individual normally spends about one hour in the role of counsellor and one hour in the role of client. In this way, true interdependence is established. Neither part is wholly dependent upon the other. Responsibility is shared, though responsibility for working through problems remains firmly with the client. The counsellor may be invited to make interventions at the request of the client, according to a pre-determined contract established between them.

Co-counselling can be used in a variety of ways. It can be a means of de-stressing for counsellors and carers working in areas of high emotional involvement. The process of verbalising pent-up feelings to another person in an understanding and confidential atmosphere can be very therapeutic. Co-counselling can also be used as a means of developing self-awareness through the process of exploring inner thoughts and feelings and particularly buried emotion. It can also be used as a means of practical problem solving, of talking out personal problems and making decisions about any aspects of the person's life.

Co-counselling training usually takes place through a forty-hour training course, during the course of one week, over two weekends or through a series of evening classes. Advanced co-counselling and co-counselling teacher training courses are also organised in colleges and extramural departments of universities.

Below is a simplified map of the theory behind co-counselling. This is necessarily a simple guide to the theory and the reader is directed to the recommended reading list at the end of the book for a more thorough explanation of what is involved.

A simple map of the theory of co-counselling

1   People are potentially autonomous, self-directing, positive and able to exercise freedom of choice.
2   *However*, people are subject to a variety of stresses throughout life: early childhood experiences, partings, bereavement, difficulties in relationships, spiritual doubts and so forth.
3   Such stresses cause emotions (e.g. fear, anger, grief, embarrassment) to become 'bottled up'. This bottling up stops the person from functioning fully.
4   Through talking out and through emotional release (trembling, angry sounds, crying, laughter), those pent-up emotions may be released. Such release is therapeutic.
5   The effect of emotional release is that it generates insight and enables the person to think more clearly, to become less stressed, more autonomous and more able to take charge of her life. She feels less 'acted upon' and more able to exercise choice. She can be spontaneously positive and life asserting.
6   Co-counselling training, through working in pairs, offers people training in:

(a) listening to and giving attention to others
(b) reviewing and re-evaluating life experiences to date
(c) the release of pent-up emotion (catharsis)
(d) handling other people's catharsis

(e) problem-solving and life-planning skills
(f) self-awareness
(g) stress reduction.

The assumptions behind co-counselling are that people are potentially autonomous and able to exercise choice. Through the process of living, the individual experiences various types of stress which cause the blocking or repression of emotions. If those blocked emotions can be freed, then the person can once again be capable of making life decisions and exercising freedom of choice. Co-counselling aims at enabling the individual to express that blocked feeling and thus become more able to take charge of her life.

There are implications, here, for professional practice. As a general rule, we usually want to calm down people who are frightened, reassure those who are crying and stop people from expressing anger. Could we as counsellors and carers be trained to *enable* people to express those emotions as a therapeutic human act? In the fields of health-care practice the value of such an approach is perhaps clear: expressed emotion is presumably better than repressed emotion. Pre- and post-operative situations, before and after childbirth, following bereavement: all these situations involve emotional experiences. Counsellors and carers can be trained to help their patients to express those feelings freely rather than (a) prematurely stopping them or (b) feeling inadequate and unable to cope. Co-counselling offers one approach to coping with emotion. First, it enables the individual to experience their own emotional feelings and second, it trains people in handling other people's emotional release.

Co-counselling is a clear example of experiential learning in that it asks the individual to review past and present experience and to reconstruct their understanding in the light of the discoveries made. The co-counselling format is simple and can readily be adapted to a variety of learning situations in counsellor or carer education.

The co-counselling format can be modified in various ways. The simple pairs method can be used as an introductory activity at the start of a learning session. The group is divided into pairs and one person in each pair talks to the other about whatever is at the forefront of her mind. Her partner listens but does not comment. After five minutes, roles are reversed and the 'listener' becomes the 'talker' and vice versa. The pairs format can also be used to explore *particular* issues, e.g. the role of interpersonal skills training in counsellor or carer education – any topic that is relevant to the subject under discussion. The format offers an economical and simple method of identifying a wide range of views, thoughts, attitudes and beliefs. It also honours the *student's* views and is not heavily teacher-centred as are more traditional methods of teaching and learning.

Focusing

Eugene Gendlin did some interesting research into counselling in the 1980s when he attempted to discover what the salient features of counselling were. Out of this study, he developed a process known as focusing (Gendlin 1986). It is a method that can be used by counsellors and helpers to de-stress and/or to identify particular issues that are troubling them about a particular person they are helping. A short version of focusing can be described as follows:

1 Sit quietly and breath deeply for a while. Allow yourself to relax completely. Notice the thoughts and feelings that flood into your mind. Slowly, but without worrying too much, identify each one.
2 Having identified each thought or feeling that comes drifting into your mind, find some way of 'packaging up' each of those thoughts and feelings. Some people find it easiest to imagine actually wrapping each issue up into a parcel. Others imagine putting each item into a box and sealing it with tape. However you do it, allow each thought or feeling to be packaged in some way. Then imagine those thoughts or feelings, in their packages, laid out in front of you. Notice, too, the sense of calmness that goes with having packaged up your thoughts and feelings in this way.
3 Now, in your mind, look around at those packages and notice which one of them is calling for attention. Sometimes there will be more than one but try to focus on the one that is *most* in need.
4 Now unpack that one particular issue and allow it some breathing space. Do not immediately put a name to it or rush to 'sort it out'. Instead, allow yourself to immerse yourself in that particular issue.
5 When you have spent some minutes immersing yourself in this way, ask yourself: 'what is the *feeling* that goes with this issue? Don't rush to put a label to it: try one or two labels, tentatively at first. Allow the label to 'emerge' out of the issue. This feeling that emerges in this way can be described as the 'felt sense' of the issue or problem.

6   Once you have identified this 'felt sense' in this way, allow yourself to explore it for a while. What other feelings go with it? What other thoughts do you associate with it? And so on.

7   Once you have explored the felt sense in this way, ask yourself: what is the *nub of all this*? As you ask this, allow the real issue behind all your thoughts to emerge and to surface. Often, the nub or 'bottom line' is a quite different issue to the one that you started out with.

8   When you have identified the nub or the crux of the issue, allow yourself to explore that a little. Then identify what it is you have to do next. Do not do this too hastily. Again, try out a number of solutions before you settle on what has to be done. Do not rush to make up your mind but rather let the next step emerge of its own accord. Once you have identified the next thing that you have to do acknowledge to yourself that this is the end of the activity for the time being.

9   Allow yourself some more deep breaths. Relax quietly and then rouse yourself gently.

This approach to problem solving can be very useful when you are under stress and unable to sort out what it is that is worrying you. It is a method of allowing problems and solutions to surface of their own accord rather than one that forces the use of logical or systematic thinking. It is, perhaps, more intuitive than rational. It can also be used as a system for helping *others* to problem-solve.

Having supervision

If we do a considerable amount of counselling and helping, it is advisable to seek out a supervisor. A supervisor, in this context, is a person who usually has more experience of counselling than we do and with whom we can talk through the problems we encounter in our own counselling and helping. Such a person may be a friend or – perhaps better – a disinterested person such as a trainer or a member of a local counselling group. Seeking out the right sort of person to act as a supervisor may be difficult. It is worth bearing in mind that asking another person to act as a supervisor will mean that we are asking them to spend their time on us. It is almost as though they are acting as counsellors to us. However, there are significant gains to be had from such a relationship. A supervisor can listen to us with a certain detachment and we can be totally honest with such a person if we choose to be. The supervisor, in turn, will not usually advise us how we should proceed as counsellors but will *listen* to us and act as a sounding board in much the same was as we may act as sounding boards to our own clients.

The question of confidentiality arises out of the use of a supervisor. Clearly, we are breaking the general rule about keeping what the client says to us confidential. There are at least two ways of dealing with this. One is to be up front about the supervisory relationship and explain to clients, at the beginning of the relationship, that you will be discussing what is talked about 'in confidence' to an acknowledged, disinterested third party. The other method is to talk to the supervisor without disclosing anything of the identity of the client. On balance, the first method is probably the most ethical but much will depend on the preferences of the counsellor, the client and the supervisor.

Supervision refers to the notion of one counsellor or carer acting as a support person for another. The supervisor is one who listens to the other, allows them freedom of expression and helps in the release of pent-up emotion. The role of the supervisor can be extended to include supportive functions such as:

- teaching
- counselling
- evaluation and
- befriending.

If the role is extended in these ways, it may be necessary that the person who undertakes the role of supervisor undertakes further training in teaching and/or counselling. Sometimes, too, the relationship can be used to enhance personal management skills: self-confidence, decision making and assertiveness.

Supervision in practice

How does supervision 'work'? First of all, a commitment needs to be made between two people: the counsellor or carer and the counsellor or carer-as-supervisor. Sometimes the person acting as supervisor will be an older, more experienced person, sometimes she or he will be a peer, colleague or friend. The relationship need not be one-way. It is quite possible to set up a reciprocal supervisory relationship between two people. In this case, the two people agree to meet regularly for, say, two hours. The first hour of that time is used for one counsellor or carer to be supervised by the other. For the second hour, the roles are reversed. As we have noted, co-counselling is a process in which two people meet for a set amount of time. During half of that time, one person acts as 'counsellor' to the other's 'client'. For the other half of the time, roles are reversed.

Structure

Once agreement that the two counsellors and carers will meet has been achieved, there is need for structure. How will the time be used? For how long will the pair meet and how often? As noted above, in a reciprocal relationship, the two-hour time span is a useful one. When only one of the pair is acting as supervisor to the other, one hour is probably enough for the meeting. It is recommended that the meetings take place at weekly intervals.

It is helpful that the person acting as supervisor uses some basic counselling skills to help to structure the hour and these have been described in the previous chapter. The supervisor may further structure the supervisory session by using the time available to explore three different domains:

- How the supervisee is feeling at the moment.
- What needs to be done next.
- The supervisee's plans for the next week.

An example may help here. Sarah Jones is a district nurse in a small but busy rural area. She meets her supervisor once a week and the supervisor structures the time according to the above plan. Thus, for the first twenty minutes or so, Sarah talks through her feelings about her work, her patients and her colleagues. During this time, she is free to talk about any aspect of what has happened that week. Needless to say, the supervisory relationship must always be a confidential one.

During and towards the end of the first twenty minutes, certain important issues emerge. She reveals that she feels very angry about the way that one of her male patients has treated her on recent visits. Sarah feels that the man has been particularly rude and unpleasant. Despite being upset, she has felt, up to this point, that she should try to hide these feelings and to put on a 'professional' front. Gradually, however, she has found that the situation has become more and more stressful.

Once the particular issue has surfaced, the supervisor asks Sarah 'what has to happen next?' In the following twenty or so minutes, the pair identify what Sarah has to say or do to resolve her current situation. She realises that she needs to talk about her feelings on a regular basis.

She also comes to appreciate that she needs to become more assertive and be prepared to discuss some of her feelings with the patient in question. In the final twenty minutes of the hour, Sarah is helped to draw up a definite plan of action. She decides to continue being in supervision on a regular basis. She agrees to talk more to her husband about how she feels about her work. She also plans to discuss with her patient the way that he talks to her on visits. She realises that this will take tact and will be anxiety making for her. Sarah appreciates, though, that the situation will continue unless she takes active steps to do something about it.

This final stage may involve Sarah role-playing what she has to say to her patient and how she will broach the topic of work with her husband. This final stage is an important one. It is vital that the supervisory period is more that just a 'getting it off your chest' session. The third stage allows for practical action to be planned and taken.

Obviously, this is only *one* approach to structuring supervision and other people may do things differently. The big advantage of structure, however, is that it enables both the supervisor and the person being supervised to feel that they are using their time constructively. It is important that both feel a sense of achievement in what they are doing

Evaluation

It is a good idea for both supervisor and supervisee to regularly look back over the times they have spent together and to identify the way in which the relationship is to develop in the future. This evaluation period can be built into the overall plan of the relationship, right at its start. Thus, both parties agree that they will evaluate the effectiveness of the supervision at monthly intervals.

This raises the question of whether or not notes of the relationship should be kept. If they *are* kept, who should keep them? Again, this issue should be settled before the relationship begins. It is usually better that notes are not taken *during* meetings. Sometimes it is helpful if the counsellor or carer keeps a journal of their problems and the ways in which they were resolved. This can either be used as the basis of supervisory sessions or the counsellor or carer can keep the journal as a private and confidential recording of their progress.

Group supervision

So far the discussion has considered only the one-to-one supervisory relationship. A variation on this approach is for a small group of counsellors and carers to agree to meet once a week as a supervision group. The leadership of such a group can 'rotate'. Thus each group meeting is facilitated by a different person each week. Alternatively, the group can agree *not to have a leader*. If this leaderless approach is taken, the following 'ground rules' can help to structure group meetings and avoid their falling into silence or disarray:

- Each person should say 'I' rather than 'you', 'we' or 'people', when relating what has happened to them.
- People should talk *directly* to others. Thus, they should say 'I agree with what you say' rather than 'I agree with what Anne says'.
- Each person should take responsibility for getting what they want from the group. Do not depend on other people to make the group 'work'. Take an active part yourself.

As with one-to-one supervision, the group form of supervision can be structured by using the first twenty minutes to discuss what has happened during the week, the second twenty minutes to discuss what has to happen next and the third to draw up plans.

Supervision offers one approach to helping counsellors and carers to help themselves. If we are to avoid burnout and dissatisfaction, we all need to be able to talk through how we feel about our work, our patients, clients and our colleagues. The structure and sympathetic atmosphere of one-to-one or group supervision can do much to help counsellors and carers to 'offload' and to make practical plans for dealing with future conflict and stress.

Guarding against burnout

Burnout is the net effect of becoming emotionally exhausted through caring for others. It can be likened to an extension of 'case hardening' experienced by some health-care workers. Although not formally defined as an illness, 'symptoms' include an increasing cynicism, a desire to distance oneself from others and a general feeling of being unable to cope with other people's problems. The fact that burnout has arisen as a concept which is discussed in the literature suggests that we may have a finite capacity for 'giving' ourselves to others and that it is possible to give too much of ourselves. On the other hand, a factor which tends to counter this theory is that parents constantly look after their children's physical and emotional needs without (too often) becoming burnt out.

It does seem likely, though, that most of us have a limit to the degree to which we can invest ourselves in helping other people – particularly in the potentially emotional battle ground that counselling can become. As we have noted earlier, it is sometimes the case that what people talk about during a counselling session can rekindle old or unresolved problems of our own and that, in and of itself, is emotionally exhausting.

There may be various strategies that we can use to help prevent burnout. First, it is important, perhaps, to consider the notion of *therapeutic distance*. This refers to the position in which we stand in relation to the client and his or her problems. If we are too 'close' to the client, we are likely to become emotionally entangled in his or her problems. If we stand too far back, it is likely that we will be unable to empathise with their difficulties. The trick, if there is one, is to try to assume a position in relation to the other person from which we can, at once, stay both detached and involved. Perhaps the ability to do this grows over time. Perhaps we learn it as something of a defence mechanism for both us and our clients. Either way, it is an important position to seek and one that may involve different 'distances' with different clients. The client who seeks very close attachment to the counsellor and who has the potential to become very dependent on him or her, may require a 'further distancing' than the colder, more remote person. Much, of course, will depend on the counsellor's own capacity for emotional closeness. This, again, will vary from person to person: some people are quite happy to engage in close relationships with their clients while others prefer more of a 'cool' relationship and the same can be said about the client's needs in relation to the counselling. Thus, the question of therapeutic distance is one that is *negotiated* between counsellor and client, as the relationship develops.

Another aid in the area of burnout is developing the ability to turn off between counselling sessions. It is said that Winston Churchill, prime minister of the UK during the Second World War, claimed never to have lost a night's sleep during that war. He is reported as saying that he was able to clear everything to do with 'work' away once he had left his office. Over time it is possible for counsellors to do the same. All health-care workers will know the importance of being able to switch off after work. To take home the entirety of the problems faced in any given day would be a short recipe for burnout. The counsellor, similarly, has to learn to distance himself or herself from the problems which he or she has been listening to during counselling sessions.

There is a method for helping to facilitate this process, akin to certain forms of meditation. The method involves *consciously* turning the mind away from the counselling encounter. Try it now. It involves focusing one's attention 'out' and on an object in the room. Find an object now, look at it closely. Then try to notice everything about the object: its colour, its shape, its size, the details of it. Spend at least two minutes focusing in this way. At the end of the two minutes, notice how your thoughts have been led away from those things you were thinking about previously. This simple technique, if used regularly and between and after counselling sessions can help you to distance yourself from the potential personal trauma of the session.

Levine sums up both the problem of burnout and a dubious solution to it, thus:

> There is an ancient joke about psychotherapists which long preceded today's concern about alienation and burnout. A young analyst, frazzled at the end of each day's emotional wear and tear, enviously observed an older, more experienced colleague who seemed to leave the office at the end of each day fresh and care-free. Screwing up his courage, the younger man finally asked his more experienced colleague, 'How can you leave the office so full of energy, and so fresh after listening to all of your patients' troubles all day long?' The older man looked at his younger colleague and said, 'who listens?'
>
> (Levine 1982)

Perhaps many counsellors or helpers cope only by stopping listening: either to their clients or to themselves.

Maslach (1981) identifies three stages in the process of burnout: (1) emotional exhaustion, (2) depersonalisation and (3) feelings of reduced personal accomplishment.

Emotional exhaustion

As we have noted, caring for others can be a stressful business. The first characteristic of the onset of burnout is a sense of emotional fatigue. The carer feels that she or he has little left to give to others and begins to cope with this by gradually cutting herself or himself off from others. This leads to stage 2, the stage of depersonalisation.

Depersonalisation

In this stage, the fact of cutting oneself off from others as a coping strategy leads to a sense of alienation from others. Others are also viewed in a negative light and the counsellor or carer often begins to actively dislike those people that she or he previously cared for or worked with. It is not uncommon to hear counsellors or helpers remark in a cynical way 'this job would be O.K. if it weren't for the clients'. For the person experiencing burnout, this sentiment becomes a reality. Often the person expends a lot of energy in trying to avoid clients and other people. Sometimes this is through burying themselves in paperwork and administration. Sometimes it is by keeping appointments very brief. Overall, the feeling is one of negative attitudes towards self and others.

Reduced personal accomplishment

All of this distancing takes its toll. The person experiencing burnout ends up by feeling that they are achieving very little. In some cases this is true. In others, the negative attitudes lead to an inability to self-assess and to evaluate work outcomes. Sometimes, all past work is 'rubbished'. The burnout person comes to feel that *nothing* they have done in the field of caring has been worthwhile and that if they had previously viewed themselves as caring, they have been deluded. It is at this point that many people choose to leave the profession altogether and seek work in a situation where they can avoid others. Others learn to cope by adopting a distant or cynical approach towards other people. So what can be done?

Coping with burnout

Pines, Aronson and Kafry (1981) suggest three major strategies for coping with burnout:

* being aware of the problem
* taking responsibility for doing something about it
* achieving some degree of cognitive clarity
* developing new skills for coping.

Being aware of the problem

The first stage must be recognising that a problem exists at all. This is not always easy as the process of burnout is often so insidious. Sometimes the change of attitude in the person experiencing burnout is noted by a colleague and this offers the chance for discussion of the problem. Even then, it is common for the burntout person to deny that anything is wrong or, if there is, to see the problem as being *external* to themselves. Very often, that person's distress is displaced onto the job, the organisation or onto other people. Thus it is not uncommon to hear people suffering from this type of stress reaction claim that the organisation 'no longer cares' for them, or that 'the job has changed and isn't interesting any more'. Rarely can the person 'own' the problem and identify that whilst the job and the clients have contributed to burnout, the problem lies within. This recognition must occur if something is to change.

Taking responsibility for doing something about it

Linked to identifying that a problem exists is the recognition that if anything is to change, the person with burnout must take the initiative in doing something about it. Unfortunately, this is usually what they feel least able to do. They often feel powerless and demotivated to the point of merely being able to struggle through. This is where help from other colleagues and friends can make the difference. Talking through the issues and being heard by another person can lead the carer with burnout to the decision to change their situation.

Achieving cognitive clarity

Burnout has a distinct emotional component. As we have noted, the burntout person often feels trapped and uninterested. The point, in this stage, is to carefully itemise *exactly* what the issues are that are contributing to the state of burnout. It is never only the case that a person feels emotionally exhausted. Things are happening to them that make them feel that way. Careful analysis of what is happening in the person's life and in their work can lead to the identification of solutions. For example, at a workshop on coping with burnout, a counsellor identified the following issues that contributed to her feeling burnout:

- Working too long in one area.
- Doing two jobs: one at the NHS hospital and private work for an agency.
- Not having attended any further education courses or workshops for over two years.
- Not facing up to a clash of personalities between her and a colleague.

As a result of identifying these issues, she was able to set clearly defined aims, as follows:

- Make appointment to see manager about a change of work area.
- Cut down on private work and aim towards working at one job only.
- Write for Open University prospectus, read journals and look for a course to undertake over the following months.
- Attend a local assertiveness course, which should enable her to confront her colleague.

Developing new skills for coping

The process of gaining cognitive clarity leads to the development of ways of coping with burnout. Nothing else changes unless a behavioural change occurs. The first stage in achieving such behavioural change is the identification of clear objectives, as noted above. This is not to suggest that *everything* that contributes to a person feeling burnout can be changed but to suggest that with clear goals, some things *can* be changed. The point about such goals is that they need to be clearly stated and achievable.

Keeping up other interests

This is essential for any counsellor. Simply to 'live' counselling is probably unhealthy. It is really important to cultivate interests that have nothing to do with counselling and, perhaps, nothing to do with other people at all. For example, the reading of novels can help in removing you from a counselling frame of mind. Sports and other leisure activities serve the dual purpose of helping you to stay physically fit and, again, help you to distance yourself from counselling activities.

Keeping a sense of proportion: the larger picture

This is, perhaps, the most important aspect of preventing burnout and work overload. Someone once offered two rules for coping with stress. The first rule was to deal with the small issues first. The second was to realise that ALL issues are small issues.

This approach is concerned with keeping things in perspective and realising, that from the point of view of a larger or even personal canvas, most issues that we face in life are transitory and will pass. There are few things in a person's life that they simply *cannot* deal with at all. While there are exceptions to this and while it is acknowledged that those few exceptions can lead to serious mental breakdown, the fact remains that *most* issues are of the 'smaller' variety – even though, at the time, they seem hugely important.

This is not a recipe for adopting a 'Polyanna' approach to life or for suggesting that 'everything will work out in the end'. It is, though, a suggestion that most people can and do get through serious life crises and emerge at the other end. It is also an acknowledgement that we, as counsellors and helpers, cannot invest huge amounts of emotional energy in every crisis that a client brings to us. In fact, it can, conversely, be suggested that it may be more therapeutic that we remain a little detached and thus become something of a 'rock' on which the client can cling to during that crisis. If we and the client enter a crisis together at the same emotional pitch, we are probably going to be of little help to each other.

8 Further personal development

Self-awareness is a means of helping to cope and overcome stress in counselling and helping. It is also a remarkably difficult concept to define. Arguably, self-awareness can help us to:

- Appreciate our 'ego boundaries' – the points at which 'I' end and 'You' begin. Thus, it can help us to be clear about problems which belong to our clients and problems that are our own. It can help us to maintain an optimal psychological distance in relation to our clients: neither so close that we are over-involved, nor so far that we are unable to appreciate fully, our clients' problems.
- Self-monitor: as we begin to notice our actions and reactions, we are better able to *choose* certain lines of actions. Rather than feeling acted upon, we become able to be initiators of action: we begin to take responsibility for what we do.
- Notice when we are reaching our limits. Rather than pushing on regardless, we can begin to choose to slow down, to rest, to change direction or to engage in other behaviour. Without self-awareness, we can be 'blind' to our own actions.
- Notice physical and psychological changes. If we are not particularly self-aware, we lose touch with ourselves, both physically and psychologically. We no longer notice what is happening to our bodies. We no longer notice whether or not we are particularly fit or unfit. Nor do we tend to notice our changing moods. Self-awareness can enable us to take care of our physical fitness and can help to prevent burnout in that we take more notice of our psychological status.

Below is offered a series of exercises that can be used to explore self-awareness.

Self-awareness exercises

Exercise One

Aim of the exercise: to explore your visual field

Activity: Sit quietly and look around you. Allow your focus of attention to come to rest on various things in the room. Pay attention to each item and explore every aspect of it. As you move on to the next object, notice the differences between this object and the previous one in terms of colour, texture, shape and so forth.

Exercise Two

Aim of the exercise: to explore your senses

Activity: Allow your attention to focus on your hearing. Just sit and notice what sounds you can hear and the variety of them. Try to identify and name each of them. As you do this, notice what happens to your *other* senses. Notice, too, how long you can sustain this concentration on one particular sense. You can also try this exercise with other senses.

Exercise Three

Aim of the exercise: to explore your focus of attention

Activity: Sit quietly for a few minutes, breathing deeply. Now allow yourself to notice the focus of your attention. It may, for instance, start by being focused on your breathing. It may then shift to an aspect of the room that you are sitting in. Just allow your focus of attention to shift gently but *notice* it as it shifts. Do not attempt to control your attention: simply pay attention to where it goes. Again, notice how long you can sustain this concentration on your focus of attention.

Exercise Four

Aim of the exercise: to explore things that you choose NOT to focus on

Activity: Bearing in mind the last exercise, notice the sorts of things that you did *not* focus on. Did you, for instance, avoid focusing on certain thoughts? Did you avoid looking at certain things? Did you avoid certain noises that you thought might be distracting? As you explore these objects or sensations that you previously avoided, allow yourself to focus on them completely and notice how you feel as you do this. What do you *frequently* avoid focusing on in your life?

Exercise Five

Aim of the exercise: to explore your breathing

Activity: Sit quietly and focus your attention on your breathing. Do not attempt to change it in any way. Just notice it. How do you breath? Are your breaths deep, shallow, rapid, slow? Do you sigh a lot? Does your breathing rate change as you focus on it? Again, consider how your breathing changes in everyday life. What is your everyday breathing like?

Now allow yourself to breath more deeply. What happens to the rest of your body as you do this? Pay attention to your stomach, your chest and the muscles around your shoulders as your breathing changes and notice any changes in these areas.

Exercise Six

Aim of the exercise: to explore your thinking

Activity: Sit quietly and allow your attention to focus on your thoughts. Observe yourself thinking. Do not attempt to think about anything in particular. Instead, merely notice the ebb and flow of your thinking. Do your thoughts circle around one particular issue? Does your thinking hop from one topic to another? Just notice when one thought starts and how your mind deals with that thought. As you do this exercises, notice any changes in your breathing and in the rest of your body as your thoughts change.

Exercise Seven

Aim of the exercise: to explore topics that you avoid thinking about

Activity: This exercise is more difficult. Sit quietly and focus your attention on your thoughts. This time, allow yourself to notice any sorts of thoughts that you would normally *avoid*. Then allow those thoughts to take shape. Notice what happens to your breathing and to the rest of your body as you do this. Notice any tensions that occur as a result of your thoughts.

Now shift your attention, fairly rapidly, from those thoughts that you normally avoid, to thoughts that are more pleasant or more acceptable. Notice the changes that take place in your breathing and in your body as this occurs.

Exercise Eight

Aim of the exercise: to explore shuttling your attention between your thoughts and the outside world

Activity: Sit quietly and allow your attention to focus on your thoughts. Do not try to control them in any way but allow yourself to notice how those thoughts ebb and flow. Once you have been doing this for a few minutes, open your eyes and focus your attention on one particular object in the room. Consciously redirect your focus of attention from your thoughts to the object. As you make this switch, notice any changes in your breathing and in the rest of your body. Notice any tendency for your body to become more or less tense. Now allow your attention to remain focused on the object and explore every aspect of it. Once you have done this for a few minutes, close your eyes and allow your attention to switch back to your thoughts. Notice any changes in your body and notice, too, if you experience any difficulty in switching attention in this way. Notice whether or not you find focusing 'inwards' or 'outwards' more difficult.

Exercise Nine

Aim of the exercise: to explore your approach to these exercises

Activity: Sit quietly and notice how you *feel* about doing these exercises, so far. Are you trying hard to do them properly? Are you doing them in a slightly cynical frame of mind? Are they making you angry? Do you find them relaxing?...and so on. Do not dismiss any of these feelings but allow them to emerge fully. Now ask yourself on what occasions have you felt these sorts of feelings before. Spend a little time exploring the feelings and thoughts that emerge as a result of this activity.

Exercise Ten

Aim of the exercise: to explore awareness of the body

Activity: Allow yourself to notice any sensations in your body. Let your attention move from one part of your body to another and notice how each part feels. Are there some parts that are tense while others are relaxed? Does your breathing change as your attention moves its focus? Now allow yourself to *exaggerate* any sensations that you notice. If there is tension, increase it...if you are moving your arm or leg slightly, increase that movement. Now notice how you can take responsibility for how your body feels and that you can *choose* to relax or tense many aspects of your body. Notice those parts of the body that are fairly constantly tense.

Now reverse the procedure. Pay attention to those parts of the body in which you exaggerated a sensation and try to reverse the procedure. Thus, try to relax those parts that are tense. Stop any movement in your arms or legs. Notice what happens as you allow yourself to stop.

Exercise Eleven

Aim of the exercise: to explore your physical movements in everyday life

Activity: Choose a fairly mundane activity such as cleaning your teeth or opening an envelope. First, carry out the activity at normal speed and *notice* how you do it. Notice the amount of energy that you put into the activity and notice what muscle clusters are involved. Then, slow the activity to about half speed and notice what happens. Then try the activity again, using less effort to carry out the task. Allow yourself to notice yourself 'in action' on frequent occasions throughout the day and practise reducing the effort taken to complete various tasks. Notice when everyday tasks seem to take more effort and when they are easy to carry out. Make a note of how you are feeling when these changes occur.

Exercise Twelve

Aim of the exercise: to explore your surroundings

Activity: This is a useful activity for distracting yourself when you are under pressure or feeling particularly tense.

At some point during the day, when you are walking from one place to another or when you are just 'out for a walk', focus your attention, completely, on what is going on around you. Allow yourself to notice everything that comes into view. Notice, also, the colours, sounds, movements and so forth. Do not attempt to focus on one particular event or object but allow your attention to range over everything that is in your visual path. Notice, as you do this, how much you *usually* do *not* notice about your surroundings. Notice, too, how this activity can allow you to distance yourself from the thoughts that usually preoccupy you. This 'walking meditation' or exercise to focus the attention outside of yourself can be used consciously whenever you need some breathing space between you and what is worrying you.

Exercise Thirteen

Aim of the exercise: to explore your self-image

Activity: Sit quietly and close your eyes. Now imagine that you are looking at yourself, sitting in front of you. Form an image of yourself as you imagine yourself to be. Notice what you see. Do you like the image? Is the image as you expected it would be? Do you compare yourself to others? Is the comparison favourable or unfavourable?

Exercise Fourteen

Aim of the exercise: to explore your relationship with yourself

Activity: Sit and imagine that you are looking at yourself, sitting in front of you. Now tell yourself (silently) what you should and shouldn't do. Start each sentence with 'You should...' or 'You shouldn't...' Listen to yourself as you do this. Are you judgemental...accepting...highly critical...? What does this exercise tell you about your relationship with yourself?

Exercise Fifteen

Aim of the exercise: to explore coping with self-criticism

Activity: Repeat the first part of the previous exercise. Sit and imagine that you are sitting in front of yourself. Now tell yourself what you shouldn't do. Start each sentence with 'You shouldn't...'. Now respond to each of those statements. Again, notice the *tone* of your response. Notice any tendency to justify your position, to disregard the 'critical' part of you or to ignore it. Practise switching between the critical part of yourself and the part that answers that criticism. Notice which part feels more comfortable or which part gets the upper hand. What does this tell you about your self-criticism and your defensiveness? Are you as critical with others as you are with yourself...more so...less so...? Are the criticisms you level at others ones that you also level at yourself?

Exercise Sixteen

Aim of the exercise: to explore the present

Activity: If you have been doing a number of these exercises, stop, close your eyes and just notice what is happening to you. Notice the thoughts that are going through your mind. Notice your feelings. Notice the status of your body in terms of relaxation or tension. Now compare those thoughts, feelings and bodily sensations with the ones that you had prior to starting the exercises. Return to this exercise frequently whilst working through these activities. Try to return to it during the course of a working day and explore your current cognitive, affective and physical status. Notice how you can *modify* that status if you can become aware of it. Too often we are so taken up with what we are doing that we are unable to notice how we are thinking or feeling.

Exercise Seventeen

Aim of the exercise: to explore the way you talk to other people

Activity: Sit quietly and close your eyes. Now bring to mind a person with whom you have frequent contact. Have an imaginary conversation with that person. Continue this conversation for about a minute. Now listen to yourself. Notice your tone of voice, the content of your speech, whether or not you are open and relaxed or quiet and defensive.

Now imagine that another person has joined you. Switch the conversation to that person. Notice the change in your tone, content and status with regard to that person. Continue *that* conversation for about a minute before switching back to the first person. Notice how you feel at the *moment* of switching back. Check your thinking, your feelings and your physical status.

Now let yourself imagine a third conversation, this time with the person you feel *most comfortable with*. Notice how your tone, manner, thoughts, feelings and physical status change again. Explore what it is about this person that makes it so easy to talk to them. Now notice any similarities between this person and yourself. Finish the activity by exploring any thoughts or associations that you have during the exercise.

Exercise Eighteen

Aim of the exercise: exploring the past

Activity: Sit quietly with your eyes closed. Let your mind drift back to the past. First of all, go back about five years. What is it that comes to mind? Is the memory a pleasant or an unpleasant one? Do you enjoy the process of recalling the past? What are the worst and best things about the process?

Now go back about ten years and weigh up the pros and cons of that memory, noting, as you go, whether or not the memory is a pleasant or unpleasant one. Repeat the activity, going back a further five years each time until you are as far back as you can remember.

Finally, switch between that earliest memory and the present time...and then back again. Notice as you do this switching, the thoughts and feelings that accompany the switch. Is it an easy process to carry out? What happens to your body as you do this? Reflect on the degree to which you live in the present and the degree to which you live in the past. Notice whether or not you tend to think that the past was 'better' than the present. Notice the difference, in terms of stress, between 'then' and 'now'. Were you less or more stressed in the past? Are the things that caused you stress still the things that cause you stress today?

Exercise Nineteen

Aim of the exercise: to explore your relationship with your parents

Activity: Sit quietly with your eyes closed. Now imagine one of your parents sitting in front of you. Notice *which* parent you choose. Notice how they look as they sit in front of you. Notice how you feel as they sit there.

Now reflect on what it is you want to say to them, given that you can say anything you like. Do you want to be critical...encouraging...positive...negative. Now consider what it is (or what it was) that stops you saying those things to that parent.

Now imagine your other parent sitting in front of you. What is the difference in your feelings now that *this* parent is in front of you? What do you want to say to him or her? Which parent is easier to talk to?

Exercise Twenty

Aim of the exercise: to explore fears and needs

Activity: Sit with your eyes closed. Now make a series of state- ments that begin: 'I'm afraid to...' (followed by immediate completion of the statement). Then make a series of statements that begin: 'I'd like to...'. Which is the longer list? What differ- ences are there between the two or are the lists related? Does one particular topic recur again and again? Explore the implica- tions of these two lists and identify what you need to do to overcome the fears and satisfy the needs.

Exercise Twenty-One

Aim of the exercise: to explore likes and dislikes

Activity: Allow your attention to focus on the environment around you. Let it focus on particular objects. As you contemplate each object, say to yourself: 'I like *this* about this object...' followed by: 'I dislike *this* about this object.' Once you have done this, move on to another object and repeat the process. Notice the similarities and differences between what you like and dislike about the things around you. Notice, too, when you react very strongly for or against something. Experiment with *changing* the way you label things. For an object that you dislike, try pretending, temporarily, that you like it. Then make the statements: 'I like *this*...' and 'I dislike *this*...' about that object. What changes in your perception occur as a result of this change? What does all this tell you about how you judge things? Do you make similar sorts of judgements about *people*?

9 Concluding points

This chapter is an attempt to summarise various points made throughout the book and to identify a range of other tips that arise out of the book.

- Start by asking the client what he or she wants. Work from the position that the client will lead you to what they need.
- Be prepared to say that you 'don't know' and to find further information for the client.
- Deal with what you can. Start with the practical issues that can be resolved. Do not be tempted to play the psychiatrist or psychologist unless you are trained as one. Thus, avoid 'psychologising' too quickly.
- Be aware of your own limitations. If you are getting out of your depth, seek help.
- Be supported by others: seek supervision wherever possible.
- Keep information in the form of names, addresses and telephone numbers of helping agencies.
- Continue to explore your own view of the world and resist the temptation to believe that it is the right one.
- Do things other than counselling: keep up 'outside' interests.
- Don't be a counsellor all of the time: in particular, don't try to be a counsellor to your friends or family.
- Consider that listening may be the basis of all effective counselling.
- Read what the daily papers have to say about counselling and helping. Bear in mind that it is likely that your clients will read these too.
- Don't be too willing to disclose too much about yourself. On the other hand, be truthful when faced with direct questions. If you can't be direct and honest, how can you expect the client to be?

- Don't offer more than you can deliver. Be careful about 'promising' the client that you will be able to help them or that 'things will work out OK'. While they may well, it may not be your doing that ensures it.
- Do be prepared to accept that you cannot and will not help everyone. Ideally, you should, perhaps, start out with the view that you will do what you can and that it may or may not be enough.
- Remember that the client is a person very similar to you who, in the end, has similar problems, worries and anxieties.

References

Blackham, J.P. (1961) *Humanism*, Pelican, Harmondsworth.

British Association for Counselling (BAC) (1989a) *Invitation to Membership*, BAC, Rugby.

—— (1989b) *Code of Ethics and Practice for Counselling Skills*, BAC, Rugby.

Buber, M. (1958) *I and Thou*, Scribner, New York.

Burnard, P. (1987) 'Spiritual distress and the nursing response: theoretical considerations and helping skills', *Journal of Advanced Nursing*, 12: 377–82.

—— (1995) *Counselling Skills for Health Professionals*, 2nd edition, Chapman and Hall, London.

Campbell, A. (1984) *Paid to Help?*, SPCK, London.

Davis, H. and Fallowfield, L. (1991) 'Organizational and training issues' in H. Davis and L. Fallowfield (eds), *Counselling and Communication in Health Care*, Wiley, Chichester.

East, P. (1995) *Counselling in Medical Settings*, Open University Press, Buckingham.

Egan, G. (1990) *The Skilled Helper: a systematic approach to effective helping*, 4th edition, Brooks/Cole, Monterey, California.

Ellis, R. and McClintock, A. (1994) *If You Take My Meaning: theory into practice in human communication*, 2nd edition, Edward Arnold, London.

Geertz, C. (1966) *Anthropological Approaches to Religion*, Tavistock, London.

Hammersley, D. (1995) *Counselling People on Prescribed Drugs*, Sage, London.

Heron, J. (1986) *Six Category Intervention Analysis*, 2nd edition, Human Potential Research Project, University of Surrey, Guildford, Surrey.

—— (1989) *The Facilitators' Handbook*, Kogan Page, London.

Hesse, H. (1988) *Klingsor's Last Summer*, Triad/Paladin, London.

Hobbs, T. (1992) 'Skills in communication and counselling' in T. Hobbs (ed.) *Experiential Training: practical guidelines*, Routledge, London.

Homans, G.C. (1961) *Social Behaviour in its Elementary Forms*, Harcourt, Brace, New York.

Jung, C.G. (1976) *Modern Man in Search of a Soul*, Routledge and Kegan Paul, London.

Kagan, C., Evans, J. and Kay, B. (1986) *A Manual of Interpersonal Skills for Nurses: an experiential approach*, Harper and Row, London.

Levine, M. (1982) 'Methods or madness: on the alienation of the professional', *Journal of Community Psychology*, 10: 3–14.

Maguire, P. and Faulkner, A. (1988) 'Improving the counselling skills of doctors and nurses in cancer care', *British Medical Journal*, 297: 847–9.

Maslach, C. (1976) 'Burned out', *Human Behaviour*, 5: 16–22.

—— (1981) *Burnout: the cost of caring*, Prentice Hall, New York.

McLaren, M.C. (1998) *Interpreting Cultural Differences: the challenge of intercultural communication*, Peter Francis, Dereham, Norfolk.

McMillan, I. (1991) 'A listening ear...telephone counselling', *Nursing Times*, 87(6): 30–1.

Morrison, P. and Burnard, P. (1997) *Caring and Communicating: the interpersonal relationship in nursing*, 2nd edition, Macmillan, Basingstoke.

Newell, R. (1994) *Interviewing Skills for Nurses and Other Health Care Professionals: a structured approach*, Routledge, London.

Nurse, G. (1980) *Counselling and the Nurse*, 2nd edition, HM and M Publishers, Aylesbury.

Phillips, J. (1993) 'Counselling and the nurse', *British Journal of Theatre Nursing*, 2(10): 13–14.

Pines, A.M., Aronson, E. and Kafry, D. (1981) *Burnout: from tedium to personal growth*, The Free Press, New York.

Polit, D.F. and Hungler, B.P. (1991) *Nursing Research: principles and methods*, 4th edition, J.B. Lippincott, Philadelphia, PA.

Reich, W. (1949) *Character Analysis*, Simon and Schuster, New York.

Robinson, J.A.T. (1961) *Honest to God*, SCM, London.

Rogers, C.R. (1967) *On Becoming a Person: a psychotherapist's view of psychotherapy*, Constable, London.

Sartre, J-P. (1952) *Existentialism and Humanism*, Methuen, London.

Self, W. (1994) *My Idea of Fun*, Penguin, Harmondsworth.

Sellick, K. (1991) 'Nurses' interpersonal behaviours and the development of helping skills', *International Journal of Nursing Studies*, 28: 3–11.

Speck, P. (1992) 'Managing the boundaries...using our counselling skills to help a colleague or a student can create more problems', *Nursing Times*, 88(32): 22.

Steil, L. (1991) 'Listening training: the key to success in today's organisations' in D. Borisoff and M. Purdy (eds) *Listening in Everyday Life*, University of America Press, Maryland.

Stein-Parbury, J. (1993) *Patient and Person: developing interpersonal skills in nursing*, Churchill Livingstone, Edinburgh.

Stewart, W. (1983) *Counselling in Nursing: a problem-solving approach*, Harper and Row, London.

Tillich, P. (1949) *Shaking the Foundations*, Pelican, Harmondsworth.

Truax, C.B. and Carkuff, R.R. (1967) *Towards Effective Counselling and Psychotherapy*, Aldine, Chicago.

Williams, D. (1997) *Communication Skills in Practice: a practical guide for health professionals*, Jessica Kingsley, London.

Bibliography: further reading

Abbey, D.S., Hunt, D.E. and Weiser, J.C. (1985) 'Variations on a theme by Kolb: a perspective for understanding counselling and supervision', *Counselling Psychologist*, 13: 477–501.

Adkins, W.R. (1984) 'Life skills education: a video-based counselling/learning delivery system' in D. Larson (ed.), *Teaching Psychological Skills: models for giving psychology away*, Pacific Grove, CA, Brooks/Cole.

Allcock, N. (1992) 'Teaching the skills of assessment through the use of an experiential workshop', *Nurse Education Today*, 12(4): 287–92.

Altshuler, K.Z. (1989) 'Will the psychotherapies yield different results? A look at assumptions in therapy trials', *American Journal of Psychotherapy*, 63(3): 310–20.

Anderson, B. and Anderson, W. (1985) 'Client perceptions of counselors using positive and negative self-involving statements', *Journal of Counselling Psychology*, 32: 462–5.

Anderson, M. and Gerrard, B. (1984) 'A comprehensive interpersonal skills program for nurses', *Journal of Nursing Education*, 23(8): 353–5.

Argyle, M. (1988) *Bodily Communication*, London, Routledge.

Atkins, S. and Murphy, K. (1993) 'Critical thinking: a foundation for consumer-focused care', *Journal of Continuing Education in Nursing*, 18(8): 1,188–92.

Bachelor, A. (1988) 'How clients perceive therapist empathy: a content analysis of "received" empathy', *Psychotherapy*, 25: 277–40.

Barkham, M., Shapiro, D.A. and Firth-Cozens, J. (1989) 'Personal questionnaire changes in prescriptive vs. exploratory psychotherapy', *British Journal of Clinical Psychology*, 28: 97–107.

Barkham, M.J. and Shapiro, D.A. (1986) 'Counselor verbal response modes and experienced empathy', *Journal of Counselling Psychology*, 33 (1): 3–10.

Barrett-Lennard, G.T. (1981) 'The empathy cycle – refinement of a nuclear concept', *Journal of Counselling Psychology*, 28: 91–100.

Baruth, L.G. (1987) *An Introduction to the Counselling Profession*, Englewood Cliffs, New Jersey, Prentice Hall.

Benjamin, A. (1981) *The Helping Interview*, 3rd edition, Boston, Houghton Mifflin.

Berger, D.M. (1984) 'On the way to empathic understanding', *American Journal of Psychotherapy*, 38: 111–20.

Binder, J.L. (1993) 'Observations on the training of therapists in time-limited dynamic psychotherapy', *Psychotherapy*, 30(4): 592–8.

Bohart, A.C. (1988) 'Empathy: client-centred and psychoanalytic', *American Psychologist*, 43: 667–8.

Bond, T. (1993) *Standards and Ethics for Counselling in Action*, London, Sage.

Bor, R. and Watts, M. (1993) 'Talking to patients about sexual matters', *British Journal of Nursing*, 2(13): 657–61.

Bozarth, J.D. (1984) 'Beyond reflection: emergent modes of empthy' in R. Levant and J. Shlien (eds) *Client-Centred Therapy and the Person-Centered Approach: new directions in theory, research and practice*, New York, Praeger, pp. 59–75.

Brammer, L.M, Shrostrom E. and Abrego, P. (1988) *Therapeutic Psychology: fundamentals of counselling and psychotherapy*, Englewood Cliffs, NJ, Prentice-Hall.

Brammer, L.M. (1988) *The Helping Relationship: process and skills*, Englewood Cliffs, NJ, Prentice-Hall.

Brandon, D. (1991) 'Counselling mentally ill people', *Nursing Standard*, 6(7): 32–3.

Brookfield, S. (1993) 'On impostorship, cultural suicide and other dangers: how nurses learn critical thinking', *Journal of Continuing Education in Nursing*, 24(5): 197–205.

Buchan, R. (1991) 'An integrated model of counselling', *Senior Nurse*, 11(4): 32–3.

Buckroyd, J. and Smith, E. (1990) 'Learning to help...teaching counselling', *Nursing Times*, 86(35): 54–7.

Budman, S.H. and Gurman, A.S. (1988) *Theory and Practice of Brief Therapy*, New York, Guilford Press.

Burke, J.F. (1989) *Contemporary Approaches to Psychotherapy and Counselling: the self-regulation and maturity model*, Pacific Grove, CA, Brooks/Cole.

Byrne, S. (1991) 'Counselling – an essential nursing skill', *World of Irish Nursing*, 20(4): 26–7.

Carkhuff, R.R. (1985) *PPD: Productive program development*, Amherst, MA, Human Resource Development Press.

—— (1987) *The Art of Helping*, 6th edition, Amherst, MA, Human Resource Development Press.

Chateauvert, M., Duffie, A. and Gilmore, N. (1991) 'Human immunodeficiency virus antibody testing: counselling guidelines from the Canadian Medical Association', *Patient Education and Counselling*, 18(1): 35–49.

Clark, D. (1991) 'Guidance, counselling therapy: responses to "marital problems" 1950–90', *Sociological Review*, 39: 765–98.

Clark, J.M., Hopper, L. and Jesson, A. (1991) 'Communication skills: progression to counselling', *Nursing Times*, 87(8): 41–3.

Clift, I. and Magee, T. (1992) 'Developing a new counselling course', *Nursing Standard*, 6(18): 34–6.

Combs, A.W. (1986) 'What makes a good helper? A person-centred approach' *Person-Centered Review*, 1: 51–61.

Confer, W.N. (1987) *Intuitive psychotherapy: the role of creative therapeutic intervention*, New York, Human Sciences Press.

Conyne, R.K. (1987) *Primary Preventive Counselling*, Muncie, IN, Accelerated Development.

Corey, G., Corey, M.S. and Callanan, P. (1988) *Issues and Ethics in the Helping Professions*, 3rd edition, Pacific Grove, CA, Brooks/Cole.

Corsini, R. and Wedding, D (1989) *Current Psychotherapies*, 4th edition, Itasca, IL, F.E. Peacock.

Cramer, D. (1992) *Personality and Psychotherapy: Theory, Practice and Research*, Buckingham, Open University Press.

Crits-Christoph, P., Baranackie, K. and Kurcias, J. (1991) 'Meta-analysis of therapist effects in psychotherapy outcome studies', *Psychological Testing*, 3rd edition, New York, Harper and Row.

Curtis, T. and Kibler, S. (1990) 'Counselling in cancer care', *Nursing Times*, 86(51): 25–7.

Daly, M.J. and Burton, R.L. (1983) 'Self-esteem and irrational beliefs: An exploratory investigation with implications for counselling', *Journal of Counselling Psychology*, 30: 361–6.

Daniel, C. (1992) 'Counselling sexual abuse survivors', *Nursing Standard*, 6(46): 28–31.

Davies, J.M. (1991) 'A behavioural model for counselling the nursing mother', *Breastfeeding Review*, 2(4): 154–7.

Davison, J. (1992) 'Approach with care...individual or group counselling', *Nursing Times*, 88(8): 38–9.

Debord, J.B. (1989) 'Paradoxical interventions: a review of the recent literature', *Journal of Counselling and Development*, 67: 394–8.

Denelsky, G.Y. and Boat, B.W. (1986) 'A coping skills model of psychological diagnosis and treatment', *Professional Psychology: Research and Practice*, 17: 322–30.

Denton, P.L. (1992) 'Teaching interpersonal skills with videotape...to chronically ill psychiatric clients', *Occupational Therapy in Mental Health*, 2(4): 17–34.

Derlega, V.J. and Berg, J.H. (1987) *Self-disclosure: theory, research, and therapy*, New York, Plenum.

Dillon, J.T. (1990) *The Practice of Questioning*, London, Routledge.

Dobson, K.S. and Shaw, B.F. (1993) 'The training of cognitive therapists: what have we learned from treatment manuals?', *Psychotherapy*, 30(4): 573–7.

Donley, R.J., Horan, J.J. and DeShong, R.L. (1989) 'The effect of several self-disclosure permutations on counselling process and outcome', *Journal of Counselling and Development*, 67: 408–12.

Dorn, F.J. (1984) *Counselling as Applied Social Psychology: an introduction to the social influence model*, Springfield, IL, Charles C. Thomas.

Doust, M. (1991) 'Student nurses and counselling services', *Nursing Standard*, 5(15/16): 35–7.

Dryden, W. and Ellis, A. (1986) 'Rational-emotive therapy' in W. Dryden and W.L. Golden (eds) *Cognitive-Behavioural Approaches to Psychotherapy*, London, Harper and Row.

Dryden, W. and Yankura, J (1992) *Daring to be Myself*, Buckingham, Open University Press.

Dryden, W. and Trower, P. (eds) (1988) *Developments in Cognitive Psychotherapy*, Newbury Park, CA, Sage Publications.

Dubrin, A.J. (1987) *The Last Straw: how to benefit from trigger events in your life*, Springfield, IL, Charles C. Thomas.

Eisenberg, N. and Strayer, J. (eds) (1987) *Empathy and its Development*, New York, Cambridge University Press.

Elliott, R. (1986) 'Interpersonal Process Recall (IPR) as a psychotherapy process research method' in L.S. Greenberg and W.M. Pinsof (eds), *The Psychotherapeutic Process: A Research Handbook*, New York, Guilford Press, pp. 249–86.

Elliott, R. and James, E. (1989) 'Varieties of client experience in psychotherapy: an analysis of the literature', *Clinical Psychology Review*, 9: 443–67.

Elliott, R. and Shapiro, D.A. (1992) 'Client and therapist as analysts of significant events' in S.G. Toukmanian and D.L. Rennie (eds), *Psychotherapy Process Research: paradigmatic and narrative approaches*, London, Sage, pp. 163–86.

Ellis, A. (1983) 'How to deal with your most difficult client: you', *Journal of Rational-Emotive Therapy*, 1: 3–8.

Ellis, A. and Dryden, W. (1987) *The Practice of Rational-Emotive Therapy*, New York, Springer.

Ellis, C. (1993) 'Incorporating the affective domain into staff development programs', *Journal of Nursing Staff Development*, 9(3): 127–30.

Ellis, R. and Whittington, D. (eds) (1983) *New Directions in Social Skills Training*, Croom Helm, London.

Emery, E.E. (1987) 'Empathy: psychoanalytic and client-centred', *American Psychologist*, 42: 513–15.

Erskine, R. and Moursund, J. (1988) *Integrative Psychotherapy in Action*, Newbury Park, CA, Sage Publications.

Evans, M.L. (1989) 'Simulations: their selection and use in developing nursing competencies', *Journal of Nursing Staff Development*, 5(2): 65–9.

Eysenck, H.J. (1992) 'The outcome problem in psychotherapy' in W. Dryden and C. Feltham (eds), *Psychotherapy and its Discontents*, Buckingham, Open University Press, pp. 100–23.

Farley, R.C. and Baker, A.J. (1987) 'Training on selected self-management techniques and the generalization and maintenance of interpersonal skills for registered nurse students', *Journal of Nursing Education*, 26(3): 104–7.

Firestone, R.W. (1988) *A Psychotherapeutic Approach to Self-Destructive Behaviour*, New York, Human Sciences Press.

Fisch, R., Weakland, J. and Segal, L. (1985) *The Tactics of Change: doing therapy briefly*, San Francisco, Jossey-Bass.

Garfield, S.L. and Bergin, A.E. (1994) 'Introduction and historical overview' in A.E. Bergin and S.L. Garfield (eds), *Handbook of Psychotherapy and Behaviour Change*, 4th edition, Chichester, Wiley, pp. 3–8.

Gelatt, H.B. (1989) 'Positive uncertainty: a new decision-making framework for counselling', *Journal of Counselling Psychology*, 36: 252–6.

Gendlin, E.T. (1986) 'What comes after traditional psychotherapy research?', *American Psychologist*, 41: 131–6.

Gibson, R.L. and Mitchell, M.H. (1986) *Introduction to Counselling and Guidance*, Collier Macmillan, London.

Gilbey, V. (1990) 'Screening and counselling clinic evaluation project', *Canadian Journal of Nursing Research*, 22(3): 23–38.

Gillam, T. (1993) 'Representational systems in counselling', *Nursing Standard*, 8(10): 25–7.

Goldfried, M.R., Greenberg, L.S. and Marmar, C. (1990) 'Individual psychotherapy: process and outcome', *Annual Review of Psychology*, 41: 659–88.

Gould, D. (1990) 'Empathy: a review of the literature with suggestions for an alternative research strategy', *Journal of Advanced Nursing*, 15(10): 1,167–74.

Greenberg, L.S. (1992) 'Task analysis: identifying components of interpersonal conflict resolution' in S.G. Toukmanian and D.L. Rennie (eds), *Psychotherapy Process Research: paradigmatic and narrative approaches*, London, Sage, pp. 22–50.

Greenberg, L.S. and Pinsof, W.M. (eds) (1986) *The Psychotherapeutic Process: a research handbook*, New York, Guildford Press.

Grencavage, L.N. and Norcross, J.C. (1990) 'Where are the commonalities among the therapeutic common factors?', *Professional Psychology: research and practice*, 21: 372–8.

Guccione, A.A. and DeMont, M.E. (1987) 'Interpersonal skills education in entry-level physical therapy programs', *Physical Therapy*, 67(3): 388–93.

Hardin, S.I., Subich, L.M. and Holvey, J.M. (1988) 'Expectancies for counselling in relation to premature termination', *Journal of Counselling Psychology*, 35: 37–40.

Hare, A.P. (1976) *Handbook of Small Group Research*, New York, Free Press.

Hargie, O. (ed.) (1986) *A Handbook of Communication Skills*, London, Croom Helm.

Hasler, K. (1993) 'Bereavement counselling,' *Nursing Standard*, 7(40): 31–6.

Henry, W.P., Strupp, H.H., Schact, T.E. and Gaston, L. (1994) 'Psychodynamic approaches' in A.E. Bergin and S.L. Garfield (eds) *Handbook of Psychotherapy and Behaviour Change*, 4th edition, New York, Wiley, pp. 467–508.

Heppner, P.P. (1989) 'Identifying the complexities within clients' thinking and decision making', *Journal of Counselling Psychology*, 36: 257–9.

Heppner, P.P. and Krauskopf, C.J. (1987) 'An information-processing approach to personal problem solving', *Counselling Psychologist*, 15: 371–447.

Heppner, P.P., Kivlighan Jr., D.M. and Wampold, B.E. (1992) *Research Design in Counselling*, Pacific Grove, CA, Brooks/Cole.

Hill, C.E. and Corbett, M.M. (1993) 'A perspective on the history of process and outcome research in counselling psychology', *Journal of Counselling Psychology*, 32: 3–22.

Hill, C.E. (1989) *Therapist Techniques and Client Outcomes: eight cases of brief psychotherapy*, London, Sage.

—— (1991) 'Almost everything you ever wanted to know about how to do process research on counselling and psychotherapy but didn't know who to ask' in C.E. Watkins and L.J. Schneider (eds), *Research in Counselling*, Hillsdale, NJ, Lawrence Erlbaum, pp. 85–118.

Hopper, E. (1991) 'Shattered dreams...counselling work with bereaved parents', *Nursing Standard*, 6(4): 20–1.

Hunt, P. (1985) *Clients' Responses to Marriage Counselling*, Rugby, NMGC.

Ivey, A.E. (1987) *Counselling and Psychotherapy: skills, theories and practice*, London, Prentice Hall International.

Jacob, M.R. (1988) 'Putting research into practice: the impact of interpersonal skills training on responses to patients' emotional concerns by nursing staff in a general hospital', *Florida Nurse*, 36(9): 18.

Jeavons, B. (1991) 'Developing counselling skills', *Nursing (London), The Journal of Clinical Practice Education and Management*, 4(38): 28–9.

Johnson, D.W. and Johnson, F.P. (1982) *Joining Together*, 2nd edition, Englewood Cliffs, New Jersey, Prentice Hall.

Jones, A. (1992) 'Confronting the inevitable...counselling...a patient', *Nursing Standard*, 6(46): 54–6.

Kazdin, A.E. (1994) 'Methodology, design and evaluation in psychotherapy research' in A.E. Bergin and S.L. Garfield (eds) *Handbook of Psychotherapy and Behaviour Change*, 4th edition, Chichester, Wiley, pp. 19–71.

Kottler, J.A. (1986) *On Being a Therapist*, San Francisco, Jossey-Bass.

Lambert, M.J., Masters, K.S. and Ogles, B.M. (1991) 'Outcome research in counselling' in C.E. Watkins and L.J. Schneider (eds), *Research in Counselling*, Hillsdale, NJ, Lawrence Erlbaum, pp. 51–84.

Larson, V.A. (1987) 'An exploration of psychotherapeutic resonance', *Psychotherapy*, 24: 321–4.

Lietaer, G. (1992) 'Helping and hindering processes in client-centred/experiential psychotherapy: a content analysis of client and therapist postsession perceptions' in S.G. Toukmanian and D.L. Rennie (eds) *Psychotherapy Process Research: paradigmatic and narrative approaches*, London, Sage, pp. 134–62.

—— (1991) 'Client-centred/experiential psychotherapy and counselling bibliographic survey 1988–90', *Psychotherapeutische Bijdragen*, Report No. 6.

Luborsky, L. (1984) *Principles of Psychotherapy: a manual for supportive-expressive treatment*, New York, Basic Books.

—— (1993) 'Recommendations for training therapists based on manuals for psychotherapy research', *Psychotherapy*, 30(4): 578–80.

Luborsky, L. and DeRubeis, R.J. (1984) 'The use of psychotherapy treatment manuals: a small revolution in psychotherapy research style', *Clinical Psychology Review*, 54: 39–47.

Macaskill, N. and Macaskill, A. (1992) 'Psychotherapists-in-training evaluate their personal therapy: results of a UK survey', *British Journal of Psychotherapy*, 9(2): 133–8.

Maguire, P. (1991) 'Managing difficult communication tasks' in R. Corney (ed.) *Developing Communication Skills in Medicine*, London, Routledge.

Marks, S.E. and Tolsma, R.J. (1986) 'Empathy research: some methodological considerations', *Psychotherapy*, 23: 4–20.

Marshall, E.K. and Kurtz, P.D. (eds) (1982) *Interpersonal Helping Skills: a guide to training methods, programs and resources*, Jossey Bass, San Francisco, California.

Marte, A.L. (1991) 'Experiential learning strategies for promoting positive staff attitudes toward the elderly', *Journal of Continuing Education in Nursing*, 22(2): 73–7.

Martin, J., Martin, W. and Slemon, A.G. (1989) 'Cognitive-mediational models of action-act sequences in counselling', *Journal of Counselling Psychology*, 36: 8–16.

McCamiele, R. (ed.) (1982) *Calling Education Into Account*, Heinemann, London.

McLeod, J. (1994a) 'The research agenda for counselling', *Counselling*, 5(1): 41–3.

—— (1994b) 'Issues in the organisation of counselling: learning from NMGC', *British Journal of Guidance and Counselling*, 22(2): 163–74.

McMillan, I. (1991) 'A listening ear...telephone counselling', *Nursing Times*, 87(6): 30–1.

Meara, N.M. and Thorne, B. (1988) *Person-Centred Counselling in Action*, London, Sage.

Melby, V. (1992) 'Counselling of patients with HIV related diseases: what is the role of the nurse?', *Journal of Clinical Nursing*, 1(1): 39–45.

Murgatroyd, S. and Woolfe, R. (1982) *Coping with Crisis: understanding and helping persons in need*, London, Harper and Row.

Myerscough, P.R. (1989) *Talking With Patients: a basic clinical skill*, Oxford, Oxford Medical Publications.

Neale, J. (1993) 'Emotional aspects of HIV', *Physiotherapy*, 79 (3): 173–7.

Newell, R. and Dryden, W. (1991) 'Clinical problems: an introduction to the cognitive-behavioural approach' in W. Dryden and R. Rentoul (eds) *Clinical Problems: a cognitive-behavioural approach*, London, Routledge.

Newell, R. (1994) *Interviewing Skills for Nurses and Other Health Care Professionals: a Structured Approach*, London, Routledge.

—— (1992) 'Anxiety, accuracy and reflection: the limits of professional development', *Journal of Advanced Nursing*, 17: 1,326–33.

Nkowane, A.M. (1993) 'Breaking the silence: the need for counselling of HIV/ AIDS patients', *International Nursing Review*, 40(1): 17–20, 24.

Omer, H. and Dar, R. (1992) 'Changing trends in three decades of psychotherapy research: the flight from theory into pragmatics', *Journal of Consulting and Clinical Psychology*, 60: 88–93.

Open University Coping With Crisis Group (1987) *Running Workshops: a guide for trainers in the helping professions*, Croom Helm, London.

Orlinsky, D.E. (1989) 'Researchers' images of psychotherapy: their origins and influence on research', *Clinical Psychology Review*, 9: 413–41.

Parry, G. (1992) 'Improving psychotherapy services: applications of research, audit and evaluation', *British Journal of Clinical Psychology*, 31: 3–19.

Patterson, C.H. (1984) 'Empathy, warmth and genuineness in psychotherapy: a review of reviews', *Psychotherapy*, 21: 431–8.

Paunonen, M. (1991) 'Testing a model for counsellor training in three public health-care organisations', *Nurse Education Today*, 11(4): 270–7.

Pearson, R.E. (1983) 'Support groups: a conceptualization', *Personnel and Guidance Journal*, 61: 361–4.

Pekarik, G. and Wierzbicki, M. (1986) 'The relationship between clients' expected and actual treatment duration', *Psychotherapy*, 23: 532–4.

Pope, B. (1986) *Social Skills Training for Psychiatric Nurses*, London, Harper and Row.

Reddy, M. (1987) *The Manager's Guide to Counselling at Work*, London, Methuen.

—— (1994b) 'Storytelling in psychotherapy: the client's subjective experience', *Psychotherapy*, 31: 234–43.

Richards, D.A. and McDonald, R. (1990) *Behavioural Psychotherapy: a handbook for nurses*, Oxford, Heinemann.

Satow, A. and Evans, M. (1983) *Working with Groups*, Tacade, Manchester.

Shoham-Salomon, V. and Rosenthal, R. (1987) 'Paradoxical interventions: a meta-analysis', *Journal of Consulting and Clinical Psychology*, 55: 22–8.

Skovholt, T.M. and Ronnestad, M.H. (1992) *The Evolving Professional Self: stages and themes in therapist and counselor development*, New York, Wiley.

Sloboda, J.A., Hopkins, J.S., Turner, A., Rogers, D. and McLeod, J. (1993) 'An evaluated staff counselling programme in a public sector organisation', *Employee Counselling Today*, 5(5): 4–12.

Speck, P. (1992) 'Managing the boundaries...using our counselling skills to help a colleague or a student can create more problems', *Nursing Times*, 88 (32): 22.

Steenbarger, B.N. (1992) 'Toward science-practice integration in brief counselling and psychotherapy', *Counselling Psychologist*, 20: 403–50.

Stiles, W.B., Elliott, R., Llewellyn, S., Firth-Cozens, J., Margison, F., Shapiro, D.A. and Hardy, G. (1990) 'Assimilation of problematic experiences by clients in psychotherapy', *Psychotherapy*, 27: 411–20.

Sweeney, J.A., Clarkin, J.F. and Fitzgibbon, M.L. (1987) 'Current practice of psychological assessment', *Professional Psychology: Research and Practice*, 18: 377–80.

Thorne, B. and Dryden, W. (eds) (1993) *Counselling: interdisciplinary perspectives*, Buckingham, Open University Press.

Thorne, P. (1991) 'Assessment of prior experiential learning', *Nursing Standard*, 6(10): 32–4.

Toukmanian, S.G. (1992) 'Studying the client's perceptual processes and their outcomes in psychotherapy' in S.G. Toukmanian and D.L. Rennie (eds), *Psychotherapy Process Research: Paradigmatic and Narrative Approaches*, London, Sage, pp. 77–107.

Van Deurzen-Smith, E. (1988) *Existential Counselling in Practice*, Newbury Park, CA, Sage Publications.

Vandecreek, L. and Angstadt, L. (1985) 'Client preferences and anticipations about counselor self-disclosure', *Journal of Counselling Psychology*, 32: 206–14.

Victor, C., Jefferies, S. and Sherr, L. (1993) 'Improving counselling skills: training in obstetric and paediatric HIV and AIDS', *Professional Care of Mother and Child*, 3(4): 97–100.

Wright, J. (1991) 'Counselling at the cultural interface: is getting back to roots enough?', *Journal of Advanced Nursing*, 16(1): 92–100.

Index